A COFFEE LOVER'S GUIDE
TO
COFFEE

SHLOMO STERN

A COFFEE LOVER'S GUIDE TO COFFEE
SHLOMO STERN

I am very grateful to my wife and children, whose support enabled me to complete the mission. Special thanks to my friends Mike Stern and Nili Ben-Yehezkel who devoted their time, skill and proficiency to the book. I also wish to thank Shaul and Maruwan who taught me so much about the coffee world.

1st edition published September 2006
2nd edition published July 2008

Disclaimer
The content in this book is based on personal knowledge and experience. It's not a scientific book and the information cannot be used as scientific facts. Before making any decision regarding your coffee drinking habits or regarding its effect on your health, consult a doctor.

Most of the color pictures from this book can be found at
www.coffee-lovers-guide.com
The pictures are covered by copyright and cannot
be copied or reproduced.

INTRODUCTION

In a quiet, unnoticeable revolution, multitudes of coffee shops have opened in recent years around the world. The popular instant and drip coffees have been replaced by espresso, macchiato and cappuccino – as good as those served in the best coffee shops in Italy. The expansion of a flourishing coffee market was followed by the development of espresso machines, moka pot, French press and other newfangled equipment. This rapid development created a gap between those who wanted to learn and understand the coffee world and the availability of reading material. The aim of this book is to fill that gap. I hope you'll enjoy reading this guide and that it will improve your coffee enjoyment. To all coffee lovers everywhere, cheers!

Shlomo

TABLE OF CONTENTS

TABLE OF CONTENTS

HISTORY

There are many legends about the introduction of coffee in the world. The most famous one, which was told mouth to ear from father to son, was published in the 18th century by the writer Banesius. It's the tale of a shepherd (some claim his name was Kaldi), who in the 6th century A.D. noticed that on certain nights his grazing goats would leap and dance weirdly. He asked the advice of an Imam (an Islamic religious leader). The Imam decided to observe the vegetation in the grazing field. He noticed the phenomenon occurred when the goats ate bright red berries of a certain dark-leafed shrub. The Imam gathered some of these berries, and studied them. In his experiments with the berries, he boiled them and sampled the resulting beverage. To his utmost surprise he suddenly felt vigorous and stayed awake all night without any side effects. He encouraged his followers to drink the beverage so they could pray and study long into the night.

The beverage spread from town to town, and in time people learned the source of the stimulant was in the beans and began to roast and grind them. The fruit, which originated in Africa, was smuggled to other countries by visiting sailors who had also learned of its invigorating characteristics, making it popular all over the world. The Spanish conquistadors smuggled it to South America, which then became the largest coffee producer in the world.

The first coffee shop was opened in 1475 in Constantinople, Turkey. The second wave of popularity began about 170 years later and continues today. The first Italian coffee shop was opened in 1645 and just a few short years later, the

Stand of the Trade Fair (Fiera Campionaria) of Milan in 1906

first coffee shop in England was opened. It was named Penny University because visitors could drink coffee and conduct discussions for the price of one penny. The number of new coffee shops grew so fast that by 1700 there were more than 2,000 coffee shops in England.

Several milestones in the history of coffee culture:

1672   The first coffee shop was opened in Paris.

1727   Coffee was first grown in Brazil, which has become the world's largest coffee producer.

1753   Carl Linnaeus published the first coffee variety classifications book.

1822   The first espresso machine prototype was introduced in France.

1865   James Mason invented the heated-on-fire percolator.

1890   David Strang from New Zealand patented the first instant coffee. He called it "soluble coffee."

1901   Luigi Bezzera introduced the first espresso machine,
        and in 1905 he began to produce it.

1901   Dr. Satori kato, a Japanese chemist, managed to develop
        the first instant coffee.

1903   The German Dr. Ludwig Roselius invented the first commercial
        process to produce decaffeinated coffee. The process was
        patented in 1906.

1909   George Constant Washington, an American inventor, began to
        produce instant coffee commercially.

1920   The US prohibition of alcohol led to an explosion of coffee
        consumption.

1933   The Italian Alfonso Bialetti designed the first moka pot, which soon
        became the ultimate coffee machine in Italy, and can be found in
        more than 90% of homes in Italy. It was recognized in the
        Guinness Book of Records.

1945   Achilles Gaggia improved espresso machine performance by
        increasing the pressure with a piston.

1961   The Italian company Faema introduced the E61 espresso machine
        grouphead and the electric pump, two inventions that changed
        the world of espresso machines. These inventions are still in use
        today in professional espresso machines.

1959   An American inventor K. Cyrus Melikian introduced the first pod
        idea by inserting a measured quantity of ground coffee between
        two layers of filter paper.

1965   Nestle, a Swiss company, introduce the granulated freeze-dried
        instant coffee "Nescafé Gold" that become the most common
        instant coffee in the world.

1971   The first Starbucks opened in Seattle's historic Pike Place Market.

1974   Illy, an Italian company, introduced the E.S.E (Easy Serving
        Espresso) pod that has become the worldwide standard.

1985   Saeco, an Italian company, launched the first fully automatic
        domestic use espresso machine.

FROM PLANT TO MARKET

In various countries, in many areas of the world, coffee is the only source of income. A coffee tree is fruitful about 5-6 years after it's planted. Its fruit is harvested and the beans are processed until they're ready for market. The life expectancy of a coffee tree is 20-25 years, and then they're cleared and new trees are planted.

The lives of most workers who are very poor and exploited by plantation owners, are focused on growing coffee.

The taxonomy of the Rubiaceae family was published by Carl Linnaeus (a Swedish researcher) under the title Species Plantarum in 1753. This same book is used by botanists today. The Rubiaceae family includes more than 500 genera and over 5,000 species of coffee trees. The coffee plant genus contains more than 25 species grown in different parts of the world. Coffee beans grow on bushes and on trees that can be as high as 30 ft (9 m). Generally, coffee plant leaves are green, but in some species their color varies from purple to yellow.

Arabica and Robusta are the two main commercial species of trees developed in the world. A third, Liberica, is marketed in small amounts, but is economically insignificant.

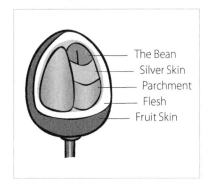

The Bean
Silver Skin
Parchment
Flesh
Fruit Skin

The fruit of the coffee tree is cherry-like and the coffee is produced from the beans inside the "cherry."

Each fruit contains two coffee beans, covered with four layers. Each bean is individually covered with a shiny greenish-yellow layer called the silver skin. The second thin, protective layer is called the parchment, which is similar to the skin of a peanut (in the peanut the skin covers both halves). The parchment is covered with a fleshy layer called "pulp" that is wrapped with the fruit outer skin.

A unique phenomenon in coffee beans is the Peaberry – a coffee fruit in which each berry fruit holds only a single small, round coffee bean. Only about 5% of the coffee cherries produce a Peaberry.

ARABICA (The Pampered Tree)

As the most common coffee tree, the Arabica is about 65% of the coffee marketed in the world. It's often called the "spoiled" coffee bean because it's very sensitive to any change in weather conditions and grows in altitudes higher than 2,600 ft (800 m).

One frosty night is enough to destroy the annual yield. It's also very sensitive

to pests and diseases, but despite all the difficulties it causes growers, it's a profitable crop.

In general, Arabica coffee quality is considered to be very high and better than that of the Robusta (however, its quality doesn't always measure up). It contains a low amount of caffeine, has a rich taste, tantalizing aroma and pleasant acidity that leaves a slight taste of caramel in the mouth. Arabica is grown mainly in South America and in eastern Africa. The two most common species of the Arabica tree are Typica and Bourbon. There's been an attempt to hybrid Arabica trees with Robusta to overcome and improve the resistance of Arabica to pests and diseases, and to introduce more vigorous species that will be more productive with an improved taste.

ROBUSTA (The Durable, "Robust" Tree)

The Robusta tree is grown mainly in Asia, South Africa and to a lesser extent, in America. It's considered a much stronger, heartier tree than the Arabica (as implied by its name). It's more resistant to diseases and pests and in some regions can reach a height of more than 26 ft (8 m).

It requires more precipitation and can be grown at sea level. The Robusta is also more resistant to weather changes than the Arabica. While Arabica beans are rectangular and elongated, the Robusta beans are small and roundish. The amount of caffeine in Robusta beans is almost twice as much as in Arabica, its taste is full and bitter, with low acidity, that leaves a slight astringent taste in the mouth.

Robusta vs Arabica

Description	Arabica	Robusta
Caffeine content	0.8 - 1.5%	1.5 - 3.8%
Taste	Acid	Bitter
Bean production per tree	0.9 - 3.3 lb (0.4 - 1.5 kg)	1.3 - 4.5 lb (0.6 - 2 kg)
Time from flowering to ripening	9 months	11 months
Flowering	After the rain	Irregular
Optimal precipitation amount	60 - 80" (1500 - 2000 mm)	80 - 120" (2000 - 3000 mm)
Optimal temperature	60-75°F (15 - 24°C)	68 - 86°F (20 - 30°C)
Optimal altitude	2,600 - 6,500 ft (800 - 2000 m)	0 - 4,000 ft (0 - 1200 m)
Resistance	Sensitive	Resistant

* A coffee tree produces good yield after 5 years.
* 5 lbs of cherries yields 1 lb of coffee beans

HARVESTING

The ripe cherry fruit is red. Not all of them ripen at the same time. Three most common methods were developed to pick the majority of the fruit at its peak of maturation and to prevent rot.

Photo: MTC group www.mtcgroup.com.au

SELECTIVE PICKING

Skilled pickers harvest the beans, moving from one tree to another, selecting and picking each ripe fruit. It requires several picking rounds to obtain the best quality beans and to complete the harvest. By using this method, growers improve the quality of marketed coffee and get maximum fruit production. However, this method is very expensive and not all growers can afford to use it.

STRIPPING

With this method, all fruit is picked in a single harvest.

Photo: Thomas Schoch, Coffee harvesting in Laos

The harvest is planned for a date in which most of the fruit will be ripened. The disadvantage of this method is that some of the fruit is unripe and some is overripe. Sorting occurs after the harvest. The fruit quality is lower and the yield is smaller than using selective harvest, but the cost is very low.

MECHANICAL HARVESTING

In this method a big dune buggy-like machine drives over the trees, grasping each one and shaking it. Only ripened fruit falls into the machine's container and the unripe fruit remains on the tree until the next harvest.

Photo: Alto Cafezal Estates Brazil

This newer method is better, the bean quality is good, and operation of the machine is very cheap. However, the machine itself is very expensive and not affordable to all growers. Even more prohibitive, it can't be operated on a mountain slope, a common coffee-growing terrain.

FRUIT PROCESSING

There are two main processing methods to extract beans from the coffee fruit – the wet and the dry process. The coffee taste is significantly affected by the method used. Each method has its advantages and disadvantages.

WASHED (WET) PROCESS

Immediately after harvest, the beans are inserted into a large water tank. The spoiled cherries float to the surface and are removed. To release the ripe beans, the dipped cherries are pulped by mechanical crushing. The released beans are covered with pulp remnants of a sticky, jelly-like wet substance. To remove the remnants, the beans are fermented in a tank for 12-36 hours. Later, they're washed again and dried for several days in the open air or by a special drying machine.

Photo: Asher Yaron www.freakcoffee.com

Photo: Parchment shell, Rich Halms, www.coffeetroupe.com

The dry beans remain coated with the parchment layer (termed "parchment coffee"). In the past, removing the parchment was done manually, but it's currently done by a peeling machine. After cleaning and sorting the beans by size, they're ready for market.

UNWASHED (DRY) PROCESS - THE NATURAL PROCESS

Drying in the sun is an age-old method, common in poor countries because it doesn't require any special appliances. It's also called natural processing. After the harvest, cherries are placed in the sun to dry in a 4" (10 cm) thick layer on a clean surface – either on roofs or an allocated concrete surface. For uniform drying, the workers frequently turn the spread beans with rakes. The drying process takes about two to three weeks. The fruit color changes to brown, its humidity drops to lower than

Photo: Drying patio, Nossa Senhora Aparecida farm, Brazil - Dallis Bros

12% and one can actually hear the movement of the beans inside the dry fruit, when shaken. Once the skin is fully dry, the pulp and parchment are removed from the bean. Because this entire process is so lengthy, the beans absorb flavor components from the fruit and taste differently than in the washed process, containing more body and lower acidity.

HONEY PROCESS OR SEMI-WASHED PROCESS

In addition to Washed and Unwashed processes there is also Honey Process or Semi-Washed Process. In this process the producer does not remove the entire mucilage layer, but dries the berries with some of the mucilage layer still surrounding the beans and they absorb part of the mucilage layer taste. This process is very delicate, the beans must be turned constantly, otherwise the mucilage will ferment and decay, a process that will destroy the beans. This process is in use on specific plantations in various countries, such as Panama, Costa Rica and Indonesia.

CLEANING AND SORTING

Photo: Bruce Edwards

The processed fruit requires a second cleaning. During harvesting the beans are picked along with branches and leaves. During the drying process, dirt and stones become mixed with the coffee fruit. And during the crushing and peeling process, broken beans and parchment remnants continue to contaminate the beans even further. First, weeds and leaves are cleared by bellows. Then the beans travel along a conveyor belt while workers on both sides remove defective coffee beans. This process is repeated once more in some places where quality standards are exceptionally stringent.

Advanced mechanical methods used in some plantations increase the productivity by 200-300-fold more than in the old manual methods.

In the current method the beans flow from a thin plastic sleeve into a glass tube in which a photoelectric system identifies defective beans, stones and other dirt pieces by their color and shape, and blows them from the tube.

Photo: Dr. Duncan Green Oxfam House

BEANS CLASSIFICATION

How do you judge good coffee? This is the million dollar question (or maybe more). Many people in the world are skilled in determining coffee quality. In the end, customers and large commercial companies make the determination, but the road to the customer is long.

Coffee, one of the leading commercial products in the world (see Coffee in the World, page 153), is spread all around the globe. Ideally, a uniform method to classify coffee would be used to allow fair trade. In World War II each country built a different classification scale. Since then, there has been no global classification system for coffee suppliers – each country uses its own method. The standard scale used by major coffee suppliers – Brazil and Colombia – was adopted by many suppliers, and is determined by the percentage of defective beans and by bean size (screen size).
Larger beans are considered of better quality. Other classification methods used by coffee merchants around the world include screening by color, defects, cultivation altitude and region of growth, flavor and more.

CLASSIFICATION BY NUMBER OF DEFECTIVE BEANS

One of the most common methods to determine coffee quality is by using a 10.6 oz (300 gr) coffee sample and measuring the amount of inedible and defective materials it contains. Each country has its own "defect" scoring table. In Brazil, for instance, one negative score is equal to one black bean or to five broken beans,

Defective beans

whereas a stone in the sample contributes two negative scores. Coffee quality is determined by the total number of negative scores. However, different scoring values are used in different places around the world.

CLASSIFIED BY SIZE - Screen Size

Beans are placed on a vibrating conveyor belt, equipped with a perforated sieve with various hole dimensions. At the beginning of the conveyor, the holes are small, getting progressively larger along the belt. The measuring unit is usually 1/64", thus referring to size 17 is 17/64" (6.75 mm).

Bean sizes range from 12-20. Generally, small beans (smaller than size 12) are unmarketable while size 20 beans are the largest. Although grading by size is common in many countries, the relation to size differs among countries. Size 17 and larger is considered the best in some countries, but will be considered only good in others.

Screen size

Zimbabwe	Kenya	India	Brazil	Colombia	Size	Measurement	
						mm	Screen 1/64"
AAA			Very Large	Maragogype	Giant	7.94	20
AAA			Extra Large	Maragogype	Very Large	7.54	19
AA	AA		Large	Supremo Screen +18	Large	7.14	18
AA	AA	A	Bold	Supremo	Large	6.75	17
AB	AB	B	Good	Excelso Extra	Medium	6.35	16
C	AB	B	Medium	Excelso EP	Small	5.95	15
TT	c	c	Small	UGQ	Very Small	5.56	14
					Not Sorted	Less than 5.5	Less than 14

CLASSIFIED BY ALTITUDE

Another sorting method is by plantation altitude above sea level – the higher the plantation, the harder the beans.

Therefore, growers use the term "bean hardness" to grade the altitude of a coffee plantation. Very hard beans, graded SHB (Strictly Hard Beans) are usually grown at an altitude higher than 4,000 ft (1,200 m) and considered the best beans.

Photo: Rictor Norton & David Allen, Rio Sereno. Coffee plantation

The coffee bean grading scale based on altitude in Costa Rica includes only two levels:
SHB – above 4,000 ft (1,200 m) altitude and SH – from 2,600-4,000 ft (800-1,200 m) altitude. The scale in Guatemala contains 8 levels.

Grading by plantation altitude in Guatemala

Grade	Plantation altitude	Grade	Plantation altitude
Good Washed	2,300 ft (700 mt)	Semi Hard Bean (S.H.)	2,600-4,000 ft (1,100-1,200 mt)
Extra Good Washed	2,300-2,800 ft (700-850 mt)	Hard Bean (H.B.)	4,000-4,600 ft (1,200-1,400 mt)
Prime Washed	2,000-3,000 ft (600-900 mt)	Fancy Hard Bean	4,900-5,300 ft (1,500-1,600 mt)
Extra Prime (E.P.)	3,000-3,600 ft (900-1,200 mt)	Strictly Hard Bean (S.H.B)	5,300-5,600 ft (1,600-1,700 mt)

TASTES OF COFFEE

It's very difficult to capture the taste of coffee verbally or in writing - just like wine. The SCAA (the Specialty Coffee Association of America@) developed a graphic tool to help cuppers define coffee flavor. It is called "The Coffee Taster's Flavor Wheel".

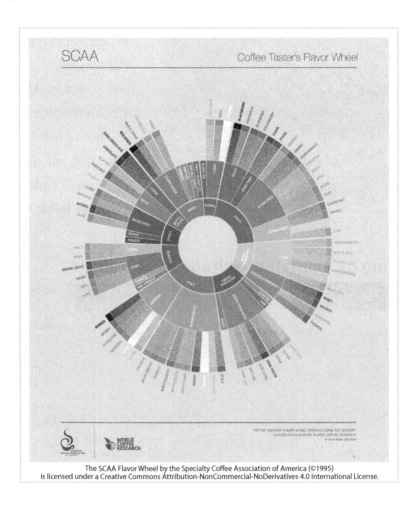

The SCAA Flavor Wheel by the Specialty Coffee Association of America (©1995) is licensed under a Creative Commons Attribution-NonCommercial-NoDerivatives 4.0 International License.

I have worked a lot with the SCAA coffee flavor wheel and I have trained cuppers to use it. The coffee flavor wheel is one of the best tools for cuppers to identify coffee flavor. For beginners or home users I have created a simple way to look at coffee taste – the coffee flavor pyramid. To simplify matters, we can divide coffee taste into two categories – the actual taste and how it feels in our mouth.

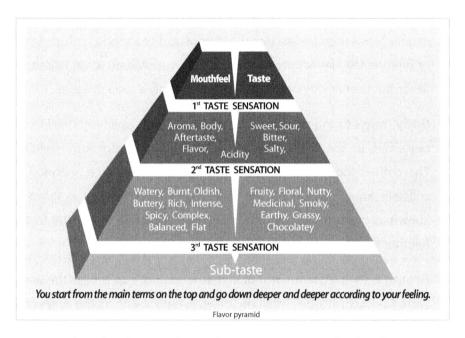

Mouthfeel | Taste

1st TASTE SENSATION

Aroma, Body, Aftertaste, Flavor, Acidity

Sweet, Sour, Bitter, Salty,

2nd TASTE SENSATION

Watery, Burnt, Oldish, Buttery, Rich, Intense, Spicy, Complex, Balanced, Flat

Fruity, Floral, Nutty, Medicinal, Smoky, Earthy, Grassy, Chocolatey

3rd TASTE SENSATION

Sub-taste

You start from the main terms on the top and go down deeper and deeper according to your feeling.

Flavor pyramid

Cuppers describe the actual taste by comparing it to the four basic tastes we know- sour, salty, sweet or bitter (the existence of "umami" as a taste is debatable, and, I think, not relevant to coffee). They also describe how the coffee feels in the mouth, in five basic terms: acidity, aroma, body, flavor and aftertaste. If cuppers want to take taste description deeper to a second level, they will compare it to fruits, flowers, nuts, etc. Professional cuppers use another third level to describe sub-flavors. For example if we taste flower, the sub-taste can be rose or jasmine.

(see Additional sub-taste Components, page 218).

- **Acidity** is the most significant coffee taste. It's also mouthfeel. It describes the coffee's crispness, not real acidity, but a feel of freshness under the tongue and inside the mouth. Comparing the acidity level between coffee varieties is fairly easy. Acidity in coffee feels delicate and soft, whereas coffee without acidity feels smooth and unified. For example, good South African Arabica coffee is very acidic and Robusta coffee from Indonesia is known for its low acidity. Coffee loses its acidity in time. Terms used to describe the level of acidity are: poor, soft, delicate or intense. Usually, acidity in the espresso cup is a good and positive flavor, but over acidity or sour coffee could imply a spoiled coffee.

- **Body** refers to the richness of coffee or to the "heaviness" (thickness) perceived in the mouth (which has nothing to do with weight). The coffee's body characteristics depend on its source. Indonesian coffee is known as "heavy," whereas coffee from Central America is known as medium and at times even light. Descriptors use the terms full, medium, light, smooth, thick, rich and deficient/poor.

- **Aroma** is the pleasant scent of coffee. When the cup is near the nose, we're flooded with the smell of coffee. Everyone knows the engulfing sense when a fresh package of coffee is opened. The terms used to describe the aroma are: juicy, spicy, floral, or even brackish and earthy.

- **Flavor** is the taste in the mouth after the acidity, aroma and body are neutralized. The terms used for better description of flavor are: piquant, chocolatey, fruity, flowery or terms describing bad coffee taste: heartburn, bitter, old, musty or moldy.

- **Aftertaste** is the lingering taste remaining in the mouth after swallowing. Sometimes it disappears after a short time and Sometimes the taste stays for quite a while.

TASTING COFFEE - CUPPING

Tasting takes coffee one step closer to the customer. This has to be done at each of the three major stages in the process: when the farmer sells the green coffee to the supplier, when the supplier sells the coffee to the dealer, and when the dealer sells it to the roaster. The tasting procedure, called "cupping," is used to classify the green beans and confirm their quality. Those are the major checkpoints, but there can also be as many as five or even seven steps in the selling process. Still, the last step is always the roaster. Although time consuming, the process ensures each purchaser they're getting the quality beans they paid for. However, despite the best efforts of coffee growers, unexpected problems can occur throughout the processing stages – prolonged fermentation, wetting the beans during transportation or other mishaps that can potentially change the quality of bean taste, even when to the eye, bean size, color and purity seem good. To decide whether or not to buy the beans and how to estimate their worth, coffee merchants are accompanied by teams of professional cuppers.

In addition, many organizations in the world conduct tasting competitions and grade the best growers and their merchandise.

In commercial cupping a small sample of green coffee beans is roasted in a small lab roaster, ground immediately, infused in just off-boiling water and tasted.

The tasting test for the end customer is somewhat different. After the beans are roasted to the required stage, they're kept for a few days before tasting.

Cupping is considered an art. The cupper must be able to taste between 20-30 types of coffee without losing the ability to recognize the unique quality of each type.

The evaluation of two cuppers is never identical, but must be very similar.

The Amazing 4 Cup Espresso Flavor Experiment

Espresso is a very complex beverage. Espresso's taste is influenced by many parameters like suitable grinding, the quality of the espresso machine, brewing time, the barista's skills and more.

One of the best ways to demonstrate the vast range of espresso flavors is the amazing "4 Cup Espresso Flavor Experiment."

Prepare one espresso shot, but instead of making it into one espresso cup, replaced the espresso cup every 6 seconds. You will get 4 espresso cups with a small amount of coffee in each one of them. Now taste them from the first cup to the last.

You will get a different taste in each cup. The taste will change from the first cup that will be intensive, full of flavor with good body and acidity - to the last one that will be watery and bitter.

Hence we can understand that when we drink a quick espresso, we actually drink a composition of all four cups.

THE CUPPING PROCESS

The table is usually set with several cups, each labeled with a number, to avoid identification of the coffee type. A sample of the roasted coffee and a sample of the green coffee bean are set in saucers for visual

impression. Every cupper receives an evaluation form for comparison in which he notes his impressions while tasting (a sample form is presented in the Appendix). When a single origin is tasted, it's customary to compare it to a known typical batch. On the other hand, in competitions, there's no need for comparison since the objective is to identify the best batches

Photo: Sarah McCans, UCDA Staff Cupping

among the cupped samples. Usually, cuppers use a flat, wide spoon made of non-reactive metal. The spoon shape increases the amount of particles spraying into the mouth with what we call a "slurping" action.

Cupping stages of the green bean:

(SCAA defined standards for professional cuppers,)

① The beans are roasted to "City" stage. (see Roasting section, page 33) between 8-12 min.

cupping roasters

② The beans are coarsely ground to French press size.

③ The cupper smells the ground coffee sample and the bouquet impression is recorded. This action is termed "dry coffee aroma."

④ A full teaspoon of coffee (8-8.5 g) is placed into a 150 ml glass. Hot filtered water just off the boil (196-203°F [91-95°C]) is added and after about three minutes, the coffee settles down and most of its particles sink to the bottom of the cup. A thin layer of ground coffee particles floats on the surface of the liquid. This is called the crust.

⑤ The cup is brought to the nose and smelled – this is called the aroma "before the break."

⑥ "Breaking the crust" – at this stage the crust is broken with a spoon, creating a "knock" of good coffee smell. The aroma released is called "after the break."

⑦ The teaspoon is washed in water and the action is repeated with each glass. The cuppers must note all their impressions on the evaluation form. (see example for Cupping Form, page 211).

⑧ At this stage the crust is removed from the coffee with a teaspoon and five minutes later, the coffee temperature has dropped until it is suitable for drinking.

---

1. scaa.org/?page=resources&d=cupping-standards

Now comes the moment of truth – the tasting! This method is known as the Three "S's": "Smell, Slurp and Spit."

All the activities are noisy and create a unique environment for coffee cuppers.

The cupper Josué Morales break the crust

- The teaspoon is filled with coffee, brought to the mouth and smelled noisily, while inhaling deeply through the nose to sense the aroma.
- The coffee is slurped noisily, accompanied by a deep inhale (very much like sipping soup without table manners). The coffee is swished around the mouth.
- The coffee is spat out into a spittoon.

9. The results of the cupping are recorded.
10. This procedure is repeated with another cup of the same batch, and in each tasting, the cupper concentrates on one taste at a time. One tasting determines the acidity and another determines the body (writing down the feeling is essential).
11. The mouth is washed with water (some claim that sparkling water is better) before another batch is tasted.

Each batch is tasted by several cuppers, and the results are compared at the end of the process. Generally, the results are different, but close enough to reach the right decision about the coffee quality.

ROASTING

Coffee's taste is affected by many factors: the type of coffee tree, the region of growth, the growing conditions, the processing method, etc. However, one of the most important factors affecting the taste of coffee is the roasting process. Roasted coffee loses  its characteristics very fast. Therefore, green coffee traded in the world exchange markets. Coffee is commonly not roasted until shortly before it's sold to the end user.

THE ROASTING PROCESS

In the roasting process the beans are heated to a high temperature and mixed constantly to obtain an even roast.

The heating is accomplished by an electric heating device, hot air or open fire. It's hard to say which method is better because each one has its advantages and disadvantages.

During this process, the beans' color changes from green to yellow, brown and even black. Then they're ground to prepare the beverage. The customer can select the stage of roasting according to his or her preference (see Roasting Stages, page 33).

Photo: Kathleen Watkins, Coffee Beans Cooling Off

The cooling process that follows is also very important. During roasting, the beans accumulate heat and if they're not cooled rapidly and uniformly after being removed from the heat source, the roasting process will continue to a more advanced stage and the beans could become burnt.

It's not recommended to use the beans immediately after roasting. Coffee beans contain carbon dioxide, which is released during the first few days after roasting.

Only after most of the carbon dioxide has been released can the coffee beans be stored in a sealed container. Roasted beans can be packaged in a special bag with a one-way valve that enables the release of carbon dioxide and prevents the penetration of oxygen.

Beans change during the roasting. They swell and lose weight, while their color and flavor change. The roasting time ranges from 5-25 minutes or even longer, and depends on several factors such as the roasting method, the appliance used, the heat provided by the roaster and the amount of beans being roasted.

When the roasting time is longer than desired, the beans are burnt and are unusable.

Changes in bean characteristics during roasting:

Acidity increases a little at the beginning of the roasting process, but after a short amount of heating, it decreases and eventually almost disappears. In parallel, the sweetness of beans increases as the sugars caramelize, but later the caramel is burned and the sweetness turns into bitterness.

Aroma increases during roasting, and begins to decrease as the roasted beans become very dark.

Body characteristics change during roasting. Figures show that body increases, but in prolonged roasting the beans lose some of their body characteristics, their unique traits and become burnt.

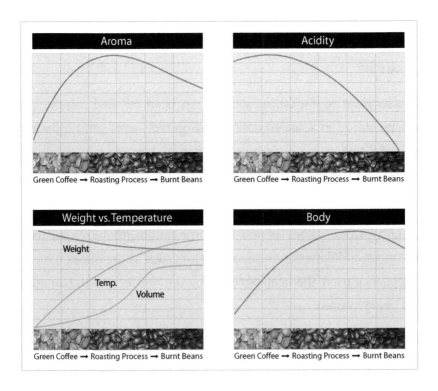

ROASTING STAGES

Roasting stages carry different names in different parts of the world. The Specialty Coffee Association of America made an attempt to agree on a unified scale using a measuring tool that evaluates color, called the Agtron. However, traditional terms continue to be used in most places around the world.

The shift from one stage to another during coffee roasting is not abrupt and depends on the roaster's considerations. There are various methods to determine roasting stages. The popular methods refer mainly to light, medium and strong roasting. In many countries, the common method used in roasting houses includes the following stages.

Green beans before roasting.

The First Stage

This is when the beans begin to accumulate heat and change their shape. While the beans heat, their color changes from green to yellow. Coloring isn't uniform as some beans are darker than others. Their odor is grassy. When the beans' temperature is above 212°F (100°C), the liquids inside the beans begin to boil, releasing steam. The sugars inside the beans begin to melt and caramelize at about 340°F (170°C).

The Cinnamon (or New England) Stage

The beans continue accumulating heat while their color changes to a shade of brown. In some varieties, the color is very similar to the color of cinnamon (the origin of the stage name).

When the internal temperature of the beans reaches 375-400°F (190-205°C), the silver skin dries and flies like chaff in the wind.

At this stage, the smell resembles toast and the acidity is at its peak.

The American Stage (First Crack)

The temperature continues to rise and at about 390-420°F (199-215°C) the beans begin to crack. The moisture inside is released and the process is accompanied by a slight explosive sound. The smell is more noticeable and the color turns to brown. The beans' volume is about 60% larger than its original size, yet they have lost about 12% of their weight.

City Roast

This roast is inspired by the immigrants of New York City. They wanted their coffee darker than regular American coffee and asked for darker beans in roasting houses. In time it became known as "City Roast." At this stage the temperature is 410-435°F (210-224°C), most of the beans have cracked and there are still slight explosive sounds that gradually stop. The color of the beans is a nice unified brown. The beans are dry, their

volume has doubled and they've lost about 14% of their original weight. Due to the drastic change in weight they move easily in the roasting container, and in air-based roasting appliances they fly in the container. The aroma at this stage is at its maximum and the acidity is still high.

Full City Roast

The temperature at this stage is 430-455°F (221-235°C). The beans begin to release oil through its skin and the process is accompanied by a slight explosion sound, similar to the explosiveness in the first crack but less noticeable. This is called the second crack. In noisy roasting devices, it's difficult to hear. The color of the beans is dark brown and the acidity is lower and balanced with the sweetness. The beans stop swelling, but have lost almost 17% of their weight.

Caution!

From this stage on, the temperature increases rapidly and the roaster must ensure the roasting stops in time.

Vienna Roast

As the temperature rises to 445-465°F (230-240°C), the beans continues to release oil. The beans are fatty and radiant. Their color is brown/black and their acidity is quite low. The sweetness is replaced by a light bitterness, the smell is unpleasant and the beans release a lot of smoke.

French / Italian Roast

When the temperature reaches 455-475°F (235-246°C) a smell of burnt oil detected.

The beans' appearance is quite similar to the Vienna stage and the only way to distinguish between these stages without a thermostat is with a good sense of smell. The acidity disappears almost entirely and only bitterness left. The beans have lost 20% of their weight.

Beyond the Last Stage

The transition between the French/Italian stage and burning is rapid and only an expert roaster can succeed in stopping the roasting in time. A very quick cooling is crucial to maintain the taste. The temperature is now close to 475°F (246°C). A strong burnt smell will fill the air. The beans oil will be burnt and the beans will be charred. The beans' taste will be carbonized and it will be very difficult to identify the coffee variety. (See Roasting Stages table, page 212).

* The roasting stages described here are suitable for home roasting. Existing industrial stages are similar, but use different temperatures.

Photo: Jos Dielis, Coffee roasting, Agro plantation, Bali

Coffee can be roasted at home by using either simple domestic or advanced professional roasting appliances.

Why roast coffee at home?

Domestic roasting is becoming increasingly popular. Actually, this is like a step back in time. At the beginning of the 20th century, roasting coffee in backyards was common, but in time most of the coffee roasting moved to roasting houses. Like many other homemade products such as bread, cakes and other food products, home coffee roasting has many advantages, but also disadvantages.

Advantages of home roasting

- **Price** - Green coffee is much cheaper than roasted coffee. The difference may be as high as five times as expensive.

- **Freshness** - Store-bought roasted coffee beans lose their freshness in a few weeks after they're roasted. While the beans can be used for a month or two, they can't compare to the taste of freshly roasted coffee. On the other hand, green coffee can be kept for several years (some claim it loses freshness after two years, and others argue it can be kept up to five years). Roasted coffee purchased in a store has an unknown roast date – sometimes more than a week previous. In addition, these beans aren't always kept under optimal conditions in the store and exposure to air and humidity can spoil them.

● **Variety** - At home, you can select and roast your favorite blend.

● **The Experience** - Not all will agree with this definition. For some it's a fault, not an advantage. However, at least some of us who like to do things ourselves will enjoy the experience of roasting and drinking home roasted coffee.

Tips for beginners:

● Coffee roasting creates a mess! The beans release quite a bit of smoke and chaff. Therefore, using the roasting appliances on a balcony or outdoors is recommended when indoor ventilation isn't available.

● Each type of bean requires different roasting times and temperatures. It's recommended that each type be roasted individually. Even in small amounts, it's preferable to roast Robusta and Arabica separately.

● Home roasting requires a great deal of organization – prepare a notebook, record the coffee variety, its weight, temperature (if possible), timing of first and second cracks and bean coloring of each batch.

● When roasting multiple batches, the appliance will become hot and the time of roasting will need to be adjusted for each batch.

● The cooling process and cooling devices are also important – a sieve and a fan must be prepared in advance to minimize the time between roasting and cooling.

● After the beans are cooled, they should be left for about 48 hours in an open jar or stored in a bag with a one-way valve to release gases before being stored in a sealed container (see Storing Coffee, page 52).

HOME ROASTING METHODS

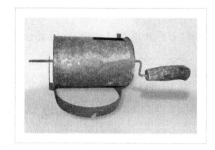

Fire Roasting - Roasting beans over a fire in the backyard was the most common method for many years. A metal cylinder was suspended over the fire and its handle was turned manually.

Surprisingly, fire roasting can create a special experience and it's recommended to those who have a yard to try it! You can use a large can or any similar container.

Advantages: It's easy, simple, cheap and fun.

Disadvantages: It's difficult to stop the roasting process at the right stage and even more difficult to repeat a successful roasting. Beware! It also creates quite a bit of dirt.

Pan Roasting - The simplest home roasting method is in a pan (preferably a deep wok-like pan). Heat the pan for about 2 minutes (without oil). Then lower the fire to medium heat and add one layer of beans. To ensure unified heating, it's

important not to use a large amount of beans. Cover the pan with a lid. Shake the pan every few seconds. Don't stop – even when you start to smell burnt toast and smoke. And don't panic, this is part of the roasting process. Because of the smoke, it's hard to observe the beans' color, even through a glass lid. About 4 minutes after beginning the process, remove the lid, mix the beans with a spatula and check the color. Repeat this action

every 30 seconds. A fan is recommended to remove the smoke. The color of the beans won't be uniform; wait until most of them reach the desired color and move on to the cooling stage. Dip the pan bottom into a large cooking pot filled with cold water and mix the beans continuously until they're cool.

It's important the beans don't get wet. The entire roasting process may take 15-20 minutes and the cooling stage about five minutes.

Advantages: It's cheap, simple and doesn't require special appliances.
Disadvantages: The process creates a lot of dirt and smoke, the roasting isn't uniform and a lot of chaff is spread around during the cooling process.

There's a special coffee roasting pan that enables mixing without lifting the lid and saves the need to shake the pan. Because the pan stays on the stove throughout the process, the roasting is more uniform.

Oven Roasting - Your oven can also be used for coffee roasting. Heat the oven to 300°F (150°C) and wait until it reaches the required temperature. Spread about 0.5 lb (230 g) of beans in single layer in a baking dish, and put it in the oven. Wait about three minutes,

then increase the temperature to 430°F (220°C). Wait three more minutes or until you hear the first crack and then increase the temperature to 480°F (250°C). From this point it's important to open the oven door every 30 seconds, mix the beans with a spatula and check the color.

When the beans are the right color, remove the baking dish immediately from the oven and cool the beans in a large sieve while mixing them. Because of the smoke and flying chaff, it's recommended to use a fan during the cooling process.

Advantages: It's cheap, simple and every home has an oven.

Disadvantages: It creates a mess in the oven, generates a lot of smoke during the roasting and chaff is scattered around during the cooling.

 **Popcorn Air Popper Roasting** - The structure of a popcorn popper and professional roaster are similar, since popcorn also requires heating of the kernels until they explode. This method is simple. The amount of coffee beans placed in the popcorn popper should be similar to the amount of corn kernels you'd use when popping popcorn. Start the machine and wait. It's recommended to use a small bowl to collect the released dirt when the popper is opened. Wait until the beans are of the desired color and immediately remove them to a sieve for cooling.

Advantages: It's cheap and simple.

Disadvantages: A very small amount of beans create a lot of dirt and smoke.

Dedicated Coffee Roasters - There are a limited number of dedicated coffee roasters. They range from small roasters for 2.8 oz (80 g) to large appliances for 2.2 lb (1 kg) and more.

For amateurs it is recommended to use appliances that provide no more than a weekly supply. It's recommended to check whether the roaster will meet your needs before purchasing.

Advantages: Does everything automatically - you set the temperature and time and you get a well-roasted coffee. No smoke, no dirt.

Disadvantages: Expensive.

Professional Coffee Roasters -
Used in roasting companies, they're available in various sizes and can hold from 33 lb (15 kg) to hundreds of pounds in each batch. Companies that produce large amounts of coffee try to increase the amount of beans and shorten

the time of each roasting cycle. Currently, hot air roasters can roast up to 770 lb (350 kg) per batch in less than five minutes.

GRINDING

Why does coffee need to be ground and what's the benefit of doing it at home? Actually, coffee can be made with whole beans, but the result would be very disappointing.

The aim of grinding is to break the hard coffee beans into small

Photo: The native mode of grinding coffee, Palestine/PD/LOC

pieces to expand their surface area. This way, the water can extract the oil thoroughly and turn it into the incredible beverage we enjoy.

GRINDING COARSENESS

One of the most important question of grinding coffee is how to grind. This depends on how you plan to use it. In a coarser grind there's less contact between the water and the coffee, and the extraction process that releases coffee oils and aroma takes longer. Higher water pressure requires finer grinding. The only exception is Turkish coffee which requires a special fine, almost powdery grind that remains at the bottom of the cup after drinking. There's no defined grind standard. Each grinder has a different grinding scale, and in time, users learn to adjust the grind according to their need.

There are four grinding levels:

- **Coarse** - The texture of the ground beans is similar to white sugar – suitable for French press and filter coffee.

- **Medium** - The texture of the ground beans is similar to table salt – suitable for moka pot (macchinetta, stove pot) and vacuum coffee.

- **Fine** - The texture is similar to ground black pepper– suitable for espresso.

- **Very Fine** - Powdery texture – suitable for Turkish coffee.

Average number of particles after grinding a single bean:

level of grinding	number of particles
Coarse	200 - 1000
Medium	1,000 - 2,000
Fine	3,000 - 4,000
Very Fine	15,000 - 35,000

Note: Grinding coarseness can be affected by weather. A finer grind is needed in dry weather and a coarser grind is required in high humidity.

COFFEE GRINDING METHODS

Many coffee grinding methods have been used since ancient times, some of which are still in use today such as a mortar and pestle. But more common today are modern, expensive commercial grinders.

 **Mortar and Pestle** - The well known grinding method, used in various places around the world but mainly in third world countries. Ancient mortars and pestles were made of granite, but they're currently made of various materials such as plastic, hardwood, stone and brass. Desert-dwelling Arabs, known as Bedouins, use heavy brass mortars and pestles. The grinding coarseness achieved with this method can be very fine, depending on the grinding time. Achieving a precisely desired coarseness requires experience. This method, based on tradition, was passed down through the generations. Rubbing the coffee between their fingers lets them know when they have reached the right coarseness.

Advantages: It's cheap, enables fine grinding that generally can't be obtained in traditional grinders, doesn't burn the coffee and can be an enjoyable leisure activity.

Disadvantages: It can take quite a while, it's noisy, creates a mess and requires physical effort.

Manual Grinder - This method is still in use today. There are many types of manual grinders on the market, and they're priced not only by their quality but also by their artistic design. For this reason, some are used mainly as decorative items. Manual grinders that are beautifully designed but not

necessarily functional can be found in many coffee shops. Usually, these grinders contain a coarseness control. The slow rotating pace prevents the coffee from burning and produces good coffee.

Advantages: A manual grinder is cheap, easy to maintain, can reach very fine grinding and won't burn the coffee.

Disadvantages: It can create quite a mess, requires certain physical effort and long grinding time, and only grinds a limited amount.

Electric Knives Grinder - This type of grinder contains two knives that rotate at high speed to crush the beans. These are very common and relatively cheap. The coarseness of the ground coffee depends on the length of operation. During the crushing process for a finer ground coffee, the temperature of the knives and the beans increase which can burn the coffee. Therefore, blade grinding isn't recommended for quick, fine grinding. Fine ground coffee can be achieved in stages, by stopping the machine every 15 seconds and letting it cool for one minute. This allows the coffee to air between stages. This machine is suitable for preparing coffee for

French press or filter method, which require a relatively coarser grind. One problem with this method is adjusting the grind coarseness, which isn't always uniform. However, because it's inexpensive and because Europeans drink mainly filter coffee, this machine is very common in Europe.

Average recommended time of usage for about 1 oz (30 g) coffee (precise grinding time depends on the power of the machine and the amount of beans):

10-15 seconds - coarse grind for press and filter coffee.

20-25 seconds - medium grind for moka pot and vacuum coffee.

30-35 seconds - fine grind for espresso machines (recommended to grind in two stages).

40 seconds and more - very fine grind for Turkish coffee (recommended to grind in two stages). There are many types of electric blade grinders on the market. Most companies that produce electric appliances also produce grinders. The difference between the grinder styles is usually in the engine power and container size.

Advantages: It's cheap, requires simple maintenance, storage and cleaning, doesn't create a mess, can provide a quick and fine grind.

Disadvantages: The biggest problem is that the coffee beans become

heated during the grinding. If you're not careful, the coffee can burn. Adjusting the thickness is difficult and the grind is not uniform (even in fine grind you'll still find coarse particles).

Burr Coffee Grinder - Many consider this is the best coffee grinder on the market, which is probably why the demand for it is constantly growing. Most of them can produce a good, uniform grinding. They feature a bean container (hopper), an adjustment button to determine the stage and time of grinding, a collection container (doser) for ground coffee, and in heavy duty grinders there's also a portion handle to dispense the ground coffee directly into the filter basket. Each pull releases coffee for one espresso shot. Some machines designed for home use are produced without the doser and transfer ground coffee directly to the filter basket. With a doser, there's no need to stand by the grinder and wait while it works, and the area around the grinder stays clean. These grinders are especially suitable for places that consume large amounts of coffee. At home, where the consumption of coffee is relatively small, leaving coffee in the hopper isn't recommended because it can become moldy. Therefore, it's recommended to use a grinder that grinds directly into the filter basket.

Operation of the grinders is based on two metal wheels, set close one against the other. One wheel is affixed to the machine and the other rotates fast above it. The wheels have small teeth that crack the beans.

Conic Burrs

Flat Burrs

There are two main types of burr grinders – flat wheel and conic burr. Coffee producers disagree on which is better. Because the conical burrs rotate slower, they don't heat the coffee and produce a more unified, finer grind. Conic knives are preferable for domestic use, but are more expensive. On the other hand, grinders with flat burrs rotate faster and produce more coffee in each cycle. There are excellent appliances available in each type and as long as the appliance works efficiently, the differences are marginal.

Burr Coffee Grinder Buying Guide

It's important to purchase the right grinder to fit your needs. There are several points to consider before making a decision:

- **Grinder type** - In general, there are three types of grinders:

  Container bin - The ground coffee is captured in a bin, allowing for a range of preparations. This is a very simple solution, but it has two drawbacks: (1) It means that the ground coffee will be less fresh, and (2) It requires manual transfer of the ground coffee to the basket.

  Doser - This is the type used by most coffee shops, where the coffee is ground into doser. Dosers allow for quick preparation of coffee as the portion is already ready to be dropped into the filter basket.

  On Demand - This is where the machine grinds the coffee directly into the filter basket. It is a bit messier than other methods, but you get the freshest grinds possible. If you typically grind small, individual portions, then this is the right grinder type for you.

- **Grinder blades diameter** - The size of burr blades affects the grinder quality. Larger blades mean a more professional grinder, with better precision and faster grinding output (measured in gram/sec. or kg/h).

- **Power** - Naturally, higher powered machines (in Watts) will produce a more professional output.

Here are some more considerations that will help you to choose your grinder:

- **Coarseness** - Can the grinder provide a very fine grind? A good grinder will be able to provide powdery grind for Turkish coffee, Most cheap grinders can't do that.

- **Grinding heat** - Do the ground coffee get heated during the grinding?

- **Disassembling/cleaning** - Check to see if the machine can be opened to clean the remains. Coffee residue can create mold in the machine.

- **Stability and weight** - Does the grinder vibrate when it works?

- **Noise** - Noise of a coffee grinder is annoying, especially early in the morning when others may still be asleep. Try listening to the noise level of several grinders before making a final purchase.

- **Grinding adjustment button** - There are 2 types of grinding settings: Stepped and stepless. It's easier to use a stepped grinder, however a stepless grinder enables precise adjustments, which is critical for espresso.

- **Portioning** - Timer or Weighing scale - If you decide to purchase an "on demand" grinder, check to see if it has a control setting such as a timer or a weighing scale. Those are useful because they grind exactly the amount required for single or double espresso shots.

- **Grinder dimensions** - Is the grinder the right size for your kitchen?

- **Dirt** - Some grinders spread ground coffee all around.

- **The bean hopper** - The size of the hopper should be suitable to your needs. It's essential the hopper closes well and that it can be easily dismantled for cleaning.

- **Service and Warranty** - Before purchasing, check how long the warranty last? Check also for service availability in your local area.

STORING

Coffee, like wine or any other organic product, loses its taste in time and can spoil. Special conditions are required to preserve coffee's flavor and aroma. The four major enemies that affect coffee "aging" are oxygen, humidity, heat and light. Exposure to each of these elements shortens the coffee's shelf life and reduces the quality of the beverage.

STORING GREEN COFFEE

The quality of green (unroasted) coffee deteriorates slowly. Coffee must be stored under dry and cool conditions. The recommended temperature is under 70°F (20°C). Exposure to the sun or moisture rapidly impacts the quality. Under good storage conditions green coffee can be preserved for up to one year. Some merchants store the coffee longer, but it reduces its quality. However, there are places in the world where green coffee is stored intentionally for several years before marketing to obtain a unique "aged" taste.

Guatemala
Antigua
Washed Arabica - HB
The washing processing results medium body, good acidity and a slight, bitter chocolate flavor with a smoky background shadow. Leaves a good flavored residue aftertaste in the mouth.

STORING ROASTED COFFEE BEANS

During the roasting process coffee beans swell and lose weight, they become less dense, and their characteristics change. Specifically, the release of oils and gases from the beans make them more sensitive to aging factors. Roasted beans can be stored for about one month in a sealed container at a low temperature. It's recommended to use a sealed bag or sealed opaque box, not a clear glass container.

Coffee beans release gases during the first few days after roasting. Keeping them in a sealed can cause the bag to inflate and burst.

Many coffee companies distribute their beans in special bags with a one-way valve to release gases emitted from the roasted beans and to prevent oxygen from penetrating the bag.

STORING GROUND COFFEE

Grinding significantly accelerates the chemical process of aging in coffee. During the grinding process the grinder breaks the hard bean peel, expands the coffee surface a thousand-fold and causes rapid oxidation of the coffee. Ground coffee loses its character within hours.

One of the best ways to store coffee (ground and beans) is the vacuum container. It features a pump that draws air out of the container to keep the coffee fresh.

This chart shows the loss rate of finely ground coffee in open air. After 10 hours, the coffee loses about 50% of its aroma.

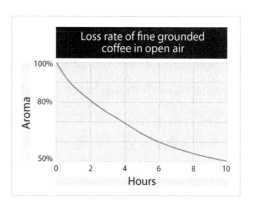

It's recommended to grind your coffee immediately before brewing, as is done in coffee shops. Ground coffee can be stored in a small sealed bag and kept up to several days in a cool dark place.

SHOULD COFFEE BE STORED IN THE FREEZER?

Many articles on this subject have been published. Some are absolutely against it and others recommend it. There's no unequivocal answer. However, there is no doubt that freezing the coffee beans will slow their deterioration and loss of aroma. On the other hand, several points should be considered before putting your coffee into a deep freeze:

- Smells and tastes of other frozen food may penetrate the coffee, if the bag is not sealed perfectly.

- When coffee is removed from the freezer, the bag is covered with condensed water drops. Opening the bag while still cold will suck humidity into the bag, accelerating the deterioration of the beans.

- Coffee beans are very hard, and frozen beans are even harder. Grinding frozen beans might damage the grinder.

Bean-freezing tips:

- Divide the beans among small sealed bags and use the coffee from one bag at a time.

- Wait several hours after taking out a bag from the freezer before opening it (it should reach room temperature).

- Using bags with a one-way valve in the freezer is **not recommended**. The coffee and cold air in the bag create suction and pressure that overcome the valve, allowing humidity and freezer smells to penetrate.

- It's not recommended to buy more beans than needed for two weeks because you don't know how long they were stored in the store.

COFFEE PACKED IN VACUUM BAGS OR CONTAINER?

Many companies sell coffee in vacuum-packed bags or containers. Shelf life of coffee in a vacuum bag is six months, and in a vacuum container up to two years. The shelf life of open vacuum-packed coffee is similar to any other ground coffee. Some companies fill the coffee containers with nitrogen, replacing the air and preventing oxidation. You should check the expiration date and keep the sealed container/bag in a cool, dark place until use. There's also an expiration date for coffee pods and capsules.

CAFFEINE

Caffeine is an energizing, tasteless and odorless component found in coffee, tea, cocoa and in other plants. In its purest form, caffeine ($C_8H_{10}N_4O_2H_2O$) is a white, solid, crystallized material, similar to steel wool.

Caffeine is known as an energy stimulator. Millions of people count on it to get them through the day. Many react differently to caffeine. Some absorb it relatively fast and the reviving effect of caffeine disappears in an hour or two. These people can drink 4-6 cups of coffee a day without any problem. Others absorb caffeine slowly, residual caffeine can be found in their blood 4 hours after consuming the drink, and they have difficulties falling asleep after just one cup. For unknown reasons, pregnant women absorb caffeine very slowly. Some researchers report that evidence of caffeine in the blood of a pregnant woman was found 18 hours after drinking coffee.

High coffee consumption isn't recommended since a high caffeine level in the blood can be toxic. Headaches, nervousness and tremors are symptoms of coffee intoxication. The maximum caffeine level recommended by health authorities for adults is 250-300 mg per day, which is about 2-3 cups of coffee. On the other hand, experts[1] agree that daily consumption shouldn't exceed 400 mg (including all other food or beverages containing caffeine such as cola, tea or chocolate).

Fact: Drinking coffee doesn't neutralize the alcohol in the blood. A drunken person remains drunk after drinking coffee and shouldn't be driving!

CAFFEINE LEVELS IN COFFEE AND IN OTHER DRINKS

The type of coffee and the brewing method determine the amount of caffeine in the drink.

There are differences between the caffeine concentrations in a variety of coffee plants. The most significant difference is between Robusta and Arabica. Robusta contains about double the caffeine of Arabica (1.7-4.0% versus 0.8-1.7%, respectively).

A few samples of caffeine rate in coffee beans:

Type of coffee	Range (%)
Decaffeinated	0.02-0.03
Brazil Santos or Bourbon	1.1-1.3
Jamaica Blue Mountain	1.22-1.23
Kenya AA	1.3-1.4
Colombia Suprimo or excelso	1.35-1.4
Vietnamese Robusta	3.1-3.2
Thai Robusta	3.7-3.9

1. EFSA Journal, Scientific Opinion on the safety of caffeine

Caffeine in common beverages:

The beverage	Amount of beverage/food	Amount of caffeine (mg)
Espresso	Espresso Cup - 1 oz (30 ml)	60-140
Turkish coffee	Small cup - 3 oz (90 ml)	60-120
French press	Cup - 6 oz (180 ml)	50-150
Filtered coffee	Cup - 6 oz (180 ml)	40-130
Instant coffee	Cup - 6 oz (180 ml)	30-120
Instant decaf	Cup - 6 oz (180 ml)	2-5
Cacao	Glass - 5 oz (150 ml)	2-20
Brewed tea	Glass - 5 oz (150 ml)	30-90
Bagged tea	Glass - 5 oz (150 ml)	25-70
Green tea	Glass - 5 oz (150 ml)	20-60
Chocolate	Pack - 3.5 oz (100 ml)	5-35
Cola	Glass - 5 oz (150 ml)	15-30
Red Bull	Can - 8 oz (240 ml)	75

Caffeine molecule:

OTHER TYPES OF COFFEE

INSTANT COFFEE

Even though instant coffee was patented in 1890 in New Zealand, it became popular only after World War II, when the world economy demanded that everything be done "faster and simpler." What could be simpler than pouring hot water into a glass with a spoonful of instant coffee? During the first years of its production, the taste of instant coffee didn't truly resemble coffee. It hardly dissolved and its commercial success was uncertain. The big breakthrough came in 1950. The taste of instant coffee improved with the invention of freeze-dried production methods. Since then the market has grown rapidly.

The number of instant coffee users increases constantly, because instant coffee maintains its taste for a long time under proper conditions. Today, decaffeinated and regular instant coffee are produced for various tastes. There are two main production methods for instant coffee: the old and simple spray-drying method and the more recent freeze-drying method.

SPRAY-DRYING

In this method, concentrated coffee solution is sprayed into the top of a high drying tower with hot air of about 135°C (280°F) flowing in from the sides. As it drops, the water evaporates due to the heat, and the dried powdered coffee is the result. This is the cheapest method, but not, by far, the best tasting.

FREEZE-DRYING

The three states of water are vapor, liquid and ice. When ice is heated under atmospheric pressure, it first turns into water and then vaporizes. However, when ice is heated under low pressure using a method known as sublimation, the ice turns directly into vapor without the liquid stage. This is the method used in freeze-drying.

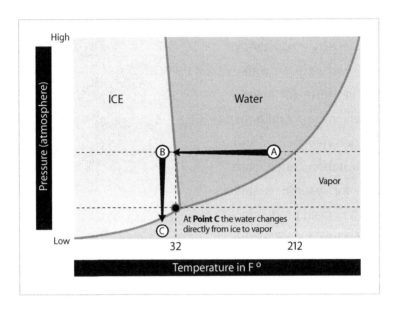

In the first stage, ground coffee is prepared in a large pot. The solution is filtered and the liquid is frozen at -40°F (-40°C).

The crystallized coffee is placed in special containers under very low pressure. Because of the low pressure, the water locked in the ice crystals evaporates and the end product is crystallized instant coffee. The major advantage of this method is the taste, which is very similar to regular coffee. Its disadvantage is the long process and the high production cost associated with the special equipment.

There's been an increased demand for decaffeinated coffee in recent years. In the U.S., coffee is considered caffeine free when at least 97% of the caffeine is removed from the beans. The caffeine removal takes place in green beans before roasting. After the removal process the beans' color changes to brownish yellow and their volume increases slightly. After a thorough wash with water, most of the caffeine has been removed but, unfortunately, a significant part of the taste components have also washed away, including the oil that contains the flavor.

The extracted caffeine is in high demand in the pharmaceutical and beverage markets.

MAIN CAFFEINE REMOVAL METHODS:

The Methylene Chloride Method

In this method the green beans are loaded into a rotating drum that blows steam over the beans, to puff them up, soften the peel and allow the caffeine to be extracted more easily. The beans are then soaked in methylene chloride – a volatile compound that binds well to caffeine. After the caffeine is absorbed, the methylene chloride is drained off. Another steam cycle follows, the remaining methylene chloride vaporizes and the beans are left clean and caffeine free.

Methylene chloride is known as a carcinogenic compound and requires extra caution. The FDA regulations[1] determine that the level of methylene chloride in decaffeinated roasted coffee should not exceed 10 ppm (parts per million). Tests show decaffeinated coffee before roasting contains

---

1. FDA, Code of Federal Regulations Title 21-Sec. 173.255 Methylene chloride.

less than 1 ppm. This method is prohibited in several countries due to the ambiguity and to protect employees from chemical exposure.

The methylene chloride method is the cheapest.

The Swiss Water Method

Developed in 1930, the Swiss Water method releases the caffeine from the beans without chemicals by using water and an active charcoal filter. Because of its eco-friendly process, it's also referred to as the natural method. Intensive advertising by the Canadian company "The Swiss Water Decaffeinated Coffee Company" made this method into a popular one worldwide, despite its high cost. In this method caffeine is removed from the beans in a complex process based on soaking the beans in sterilized 175°F (80°C) hot water. During the caffeine removal, the taste and aroma components are also extracted. The water is circulated through an active charcoal filter that absorbs only the caffeine. Later, the coffee taste and aroma components are added back into the beans in another process.

The Water-Carbon Method

This process uses two of the most important CO_2 traits – its ability to absorb caffeine and its boiling point.

The green beans are rinsed with steam to soften the peel and to ease extraction of the caffeine. The beans are then placed in a high-pressure sealed metal container that liquidizes the CO_2. As the CO_2 in liquid form is circulated through the container it absorbs caffeine from the beans. When the caffeine level in the liquid CO_2 and in the beans are balanced, the liquid CO_2 is drawn off into another container, the pressure is reduced and the liquid CO_2 evaporates, leaving the caffeine in liquid state in the container. The process is repeated until most of the caffeine is been extracted from the beans. This is the best separation method, but it's not commonly used because of its high cost.

COFFEE BREWING METHODS

Photo: Canned Muffins, Coffee Ceremony, Ethiopia

No matter which method you choose, the goal of brewing coffee is to transfer the flavor components from the ground coffee to the drink. Around the world there are many methods for making coffee. Some modern methods are from the mid 20th century and some are old, traditional methods. In many cases, making coffee is a ritual, and part of decent hosting ceremonies. Following are the main and most popular methods.

BLACK COFFEE

Black coffee or Turkish is a simple drink for the lazy, where very fine ground coffee is soaked in hot water. This is one of the simplest ways to prepare coffee at home, at work, on the road, etc. Add heaped teaspoon of coffee to a glass and pour hot water, a few seconds off-boiling, over the grounds and stir well. Add sugar according to your personal taste and after two minutes, when the coffee grounds have sunk to the bottom of the glass, the coffee is ready to drink.

TURKISH OR MIDDLE EASTERN COFFEE

An old Arab proverb says:

"black as hell, strong as death and sweet as love."

True Turkish coffee should indeed be black, strong and sweet. Turkish coffee preparation is one of the oldest methods that are still used today. In some parts of the world it's called Middle Eastern coffee and in Greece, Greek coffee, of course. Despite the many names, the preparation method is the same. Turkish coffee is prepared in a coffee pot – "Finjan" (in Arab countries), "Cezve" (in Turkey) and "Ibrik" (in Greece). Very fine ground coffee is cooked in just off-boiling water over a low fire. It's important to remove the coffee pot from the fire before the water reaches a boil. In many places in the world it's customary to add spices to the ground coffee, the most popular among them are cardamom and cinnamon, but cloves and fennel are also commonly used. The World Coffee Events Organization runs an annual championship to find the best Cezve-Ibrik maker (see Competitions & Championship, page 135).

Preparation:

1. Grind the coffee to a very fine powder to prevent floating particles.
2. Fill the Cezve with enough water for the number of cups you need, about 2 to 3 oz (60-90 ml) per cup.
3. For each cup add 1 full teaspoon of coffee.
4. Heat the water over a low fire and mix occasionally.

The water should not reach boiling point, not only to avoid overflow, but also because the coffee can burn and lose its taste and aroma.

5. When the coffee is near a boil, a light froth called "Kaimak" surrounds the Cezve walls, and advances in a circle toward its center.

6. Remove the Cezve from the fire when the diameter of the center circle without froth is about 1/2" (1 cm).

7. Add sugar according to your personal taste and stir slightly.

8. Some return the Cezve to the fire and repeat the process two times or more to increase the amount of froth (Kaimak) and increase the extraction.

9. Pour the coffee into the cups and make sure that in each cup the coffee is covered with froth.

OTHER VERSIONS OF TURKISH COFFEE ARE:

The Bedouin Version – Also Called "Bitter Coffee"

In the Bedouin tradition, coffee preparation is a serious and valued ceremony. It's important to use the right utensils and to serve it properly. The coffee is prepared in a set of four beautifully engraved pots (usually made of brass). A large one called "Dallah," a medium size pot called "Tanwa," a small pot called "Talaat," and a serving pot called "Masab," from which the coffee is poured into small China cups. Contrary to all other methods, Bedouin coffee boils a long time over the fire.

Preparation:

1. Place about 1 lb (0.5 kg) finely ground coffee into the large pot with about a gallon (4 liters) of water and put it on the coals. The coffee will boil and begin to bubble.

2. After boiling for about 15 minutes, pour the coffee into the medium pot, without the sediment.

3. Add an additional 1/2 lb (220 gr) fresh ground coffee (some add up to 1 lb) to the medium-sized pot and leave it on the coals for about half an hour.

4. Pour the coffee into the smaller pot, and from there to the beautiful serving pot.

Photo: Bedouin man in Wadi Rum grinding coffee - Jordan tour www.engagingcultures.com

When more coffee must be prepared, the large pot is emptied of coffee dregs and the sediment from the medium-sized pot is moved into the large pot. A half pound (220 gr) of fresh coffee is added to the large pot on top of the sediment and the preparation process is repeated.

This coffee is served during festivities and mourning ceremonies. If a series of pots is not available, the Bedouins use a large cooking pot.

Traditionally, Bedouins crush coffee beans with a pestle in a brass mortar and the ringing noise that sounds like rhythmic music is part of the ceremony (currently they use manual or electric grinders).

Pouring and drinking coffee are also ceremonial. It begins by pouring the coffee with the end of the spout close to the cup, then the serving pot is lifted upward creating a long, dramatic dribble into the cup. This is done to air and cool the coffee. After one to two minutes the coffee is sipped with loud slurps.

The Arabic Version

Put a full teaspoon of ground coffee in the Ibrik (also known as "Cezve"), one teaspoon of sugar (Arabic coffee is very sweet) and 1-1.5 oz (30-45 ml) water for each cup. Put the Ibrik on coals and let it heat very slowly. Occasionally check the coffee. The coffee is poured when bubbles begin to appear on the surface. Arabic coffee is served in small 3-4 oz (90-120 ml) glass cups, and only half the cup is filled. Spices, usually cardamom and sometimes a mix of Yemenite spices called Hawaij, is added to the coffee. Arabic coffee is often served with very sweet baked pastry.

Other Versions

Coffee is prepared in the same way in other countries, but with other spices replacing the cardamom such as nutmeg, rose water or cinnamon.

FILTERED COFFEE

The highest coffee consumption in the world, next to instant coffee, is filter coffee. Water at a temperature just off-boiling is dripped through the

ground coffee held in a filter, resulting in a clear and tasteful beverage. For hundreds of years, ground coffee was filtered through cloth filters (similar to tea bags). In 1908 the method of preparing coffee filters changed.

Melitta Bentz, a German housewife, invented the first paper filter to separate dregs from the beverage. She used her son's blotter paper and poured the boiling water over the ground coffee. The result was a clear, smooth beverage with a delicious taste. She and her husband developed the idea and registered a patent. Since then, disposable paper filters are one of the most common methods of preparing coffee. Melitta, her husband and the filter paper became a household brand in the coffee world. Durable metal, cotton and plastic filters developed in recent years also produce good results.

The best way to brew filter coffee – the "ideal cup," was determined by SCAE (Specialty Coffee Association) as:

Heat 0.26 gallon (1 liter) of water to 195 to 205°F (92 to 96°C) for 1.75-2.25 oz (50-65 grams) ground coffee. The balance between brewing time and coffee thickness needs to be such that 18-22% of the ground coffee particles dissolve in the water to create a drink with 1-1.5% dissolved coffee solids.

FILTER TYPES

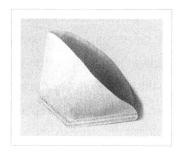

Paper Filter - This disposable filter is very popular around the world since it's very convenient and inexpensive. It's the most efficient tool for removing ground coffee particles from the beverage. It produces a clear beverage with a delicate taste. But because of the small pores in the paper, it absorbs some of the coffee oil and loses aroma.

Natural Cloth Filter - This type is produced from natural cotton (brownish-yellow in color) without bleaching. The pores in the cloth are larger than in a paper filter and remove most of the coffee particles from

the liquid. The aroma is preserved because most of the oil permeates the beverage. A cloth filter is intended for limited use, depending on its quality. After each use the coffee residue must be washed away. It's not recommended to use soap or any other detergent. In time the color of the cloth becomes darker, but it can be used until the cloth literally falls apart.

Metal Filter - This type is made of very thin metal. The most popular is the "gold" which is actually made of stainless steel that receives a unique treatment to prevent a metallic taste from transferring to the coffee. The metal filter is very thin but its pores are larger than in paper and cloth filters.

The coffee taste is richer than it is with other filters because most of the oil remains in the cup. It can be washed with soap and water or in a dishwasher. In time, after many washes, it loses its smooth shape and the quality of the coffee deteriorates because the sizes of the pores change. It's recommended to replace metal filters every six months.

FILTER COFFEE PREPARATION METHODS

There are several ways to prepare filter coffee, each has its advantages and disadvantages:

Pour-Over Conic Funnel - This is the simplest method. It's very convenient to use in the office or on the road. The paper filter is placed in the funnel atop a cup or pot. Medium ground coffee is placed inside the filter – one teaspoon for each cup of coffee and water (just off-boiling) is poured over the coffee. The brewed coffee drips through the filter and the result is a good, tasty beverage.

Pour-Over V60 Drip Device - After many years of stagnation, there has been a breakthrough in the pour-over drip coffee technique. In 2005 a Japanese company, Hario, introduced the V60 device - (due to the V shape and 60 degree angle).

This new device has rounded ribs that cause the water to spiral while flowing through the coffee grounds to get better infusion.

How to prepare good coffee by V60 device:

1. Place the dripper above the cup or the coffee pot and insert the paper filter.
2. Pour a few drops of hot water onto the paper filter, just to wet it.
3. Insert 2 teaspoon of medium ground coffee for each cup of coffee.
4. Lightly tamp the ground coffee with a spoon and make a small depression in the middle.
5. Pour a small amount of hot water 197°F (92°C) over the ground coffee for pre-infusion.
6. Wait until the coffee absorbs the water.
7. Continue to pour water slowly, in a spiral motion from the center outwards. Stop from time to time to let the water infuse.
8. The entire process should take 3 minutes.

Disposable Filter - For a quicker procedure and to make life easier for coffee lovers, several companies have produced a disposable filter that contains the proper amount of coffee needed to prepare an individual cup of regular or instant coffee. The quality of the vacuum packed filters is usually good. Each package contains several filters that should be used soon after the package is opened. Disposable filters can be kept in sealed containers for several days. It's not recommended to use the filters after the expiration date.

Automatic Drip Machine - This is a very popular method used in millions of households as well as in coffee shops, hotels and restaurants around the world, especially in the U.S. The operation of the drip coffee system is similar to that of the manual filter, but it's more convenient and keeps the coffee hot after brewing.

After filling the water and inserting a filter and ground coffee, the machine is turned on. The water is transferred from the water container to a tube passing through a heating element placed under the coffee flask. The boiling water flows up through the tube to the filter. On its way up, the cool water is heated to the exact required temperature. The hot water drips onto the coffee in the filter and permeates through it to the pot

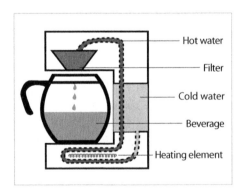

placed on the heating plate. Some people or restaurants leave the pot on the plate, for a long time, which makes the taste become acidic. Some coffee drinkers are used to that taste and even like it.

Hot water
Filter
Cold water
Beverage
Heating element

Cold Brew - In recent years, a new process of preparing coffee called cold brew has become common. It is not a cold beverage like ice coffee or granita; it is a process in which you immerse coarse ground coffee in water at room temperature for 24 hours or more and then filter it to get a sweetish delicate beverage.

A new glass device has been developed to enable preparation of the beverage by slow dripping over a period of a few hours.

In these devices the drip rate is about 40 drops a minute, which gives 400 milliliters in 3 to 4 hours. The result is a good mild coffee a little bit more acidic than the regular cold brew method.

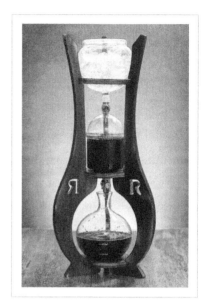

Preparation method:

- Pour 7 oz (200 grams) of coarse ground coffee into a jar.
- Add water at room temperature approximately fourfold the coffee quantity - 27 oz (0.8 liters), and stir lightly.
- Cover and leave on the counter for 24 hours. You can leave it even longer and the coffee will be more concentrated and sweeter.
- Filter the coffee first through a simple kitchen strainer and then through a paper filter. The result is a concentrated coffee which requires 50% to 80% dilution with water.
- Add hot water or cold water or even ice, milk or ice cream.
  Enjoy an amazing sweet coffee with surprising taste and unique flavor.

The French press is one of the simplest ways to prepare good coffee. The taste is similar to filter coffee. A French press is usually a cylindrical glass flask fitted with a filter plate attached to a plunger. Coarse ground coffee is soaked in hot water for a few minutes. After the water absorbs the coffee oil and aroma, the plunger is pressed down, the ground coffee sinks to the bottom and the beverage above the filter is clear and rich.

How to prepare a French press:

Caution! Preparing French press coffee requires some force and involves hot water. Therefore, when the flask is made of glass, it should be used on a dry, even surface and kept away from the face. Using extra force may crack the glass and cause injury.

1. Place the French press on a dry, even surface.
2. Remove the cover with the plunger and filter and place it aside.
3. For each cup insert a full teaspoon of coarsely ground coffee into the flask (finely ground coffee will block the filter pores making it difficult to press).

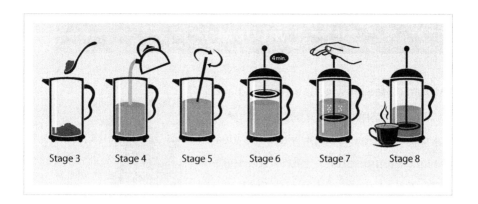

Stage 3 Stage 4 Stage 5 Stage 6 Stage 7 Stage 8

④ Pour hot water (about 30 seconds after it boils) into the flask. Don't fill it to the top. The water surface should be at least 1" (2.5 cm) below the tip of the flask.

⑤ Mix the brew gently with a spoon (in a glass flask use a wooden spoon since a metal spoon might crack the hot glass).

⑥ Replace the cover with the plunger and wait about 4 minutes until the water absorbs the aroma of the coffee.

⑦ Hold the flask steady with one hand and use the other to push the plunger gently downward to the bottom of the flask, using minimal force. It's important to push the plunger straight down and not diagonally. If it's difficult to press, don't use extreme force (this indicates the coffee grind is too fine). Remove the cover, mix the brew and restart pressing.

⑧ Pour the tasty coffee into cups.

⑨ The filter should be removed and washed well after each use.

VACUUM

Vacuum coffee brewing is an exciting and fascinating experience. The beverage is not only clear but also provides the ideal brewing temperature 190°F to 198°F (88°C-92°C). Several companies, Starbucks included, have succeeded in overcoming some of the disadvantages of the device and developed an easy-to-use electric semi-automatic device.

HISTORY OF THE VACUUM COFFEE BREWER

The earliest reference to glass vacuum pots in literature appeared in Berlin in 1830, but they didn't succeed and the patent was abandoned. A similar patent registered by Madame Jeanne Richard in 1838 also failed. Only in 1842 when a French lady named Maria Fanny or as she called herself Madame Vassieux patented a vacuum coffee brewer did the process truly

catch on. She registered the patent and immediately began to produce and sell her vacuum brewers with incredible success. She's therefore considered the inventor of this method. In the beginning, the vacuum coffee brewer was produced with various materials such as glass and metal, but today Pyrex® is the most common material used by commercial companies.

How it works

Although there are many types of vacuum brewers, they all operate in a similar way. They all have two chambers connected with a tube. One chamber is filled with cold water and the other holds coarse ground coffee. A tube that

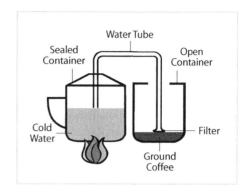

reaches almost to the bottom of the water container passes through the sealed cover of the water container into the coffee container. On the other end, there's a small filter, about 1/4" (6 mm) from the bottom of the coffee container (the cloth filter has recently been replaced by plastic).

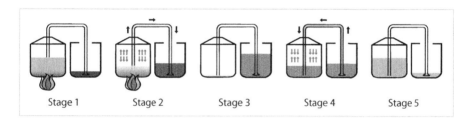

Stage 1   Stage 2   Stage 3   Stage 4   Stage 5

- **Stage 1:** The water container is heated.
- **Stage 2:** The hot water heats the air above the water surface and the nearly-boiling water is pushed through the tube into the coffee container.
- **Stage 3:** The process continues until the water container is empty and all the water is in the coffee container.
- **Stage 4:** The heating source is turned off and the water container containing mainly vapor and hot air begins to cool. This creates a vacuum that sucks the coffee back through the small filter on the tip of the tube from the coffee container into the clean water container.
- **Stage 5:** After all the coffee has been sucked back into the container, the cover is opened, the tube is removed and the coffee is poured.

In recent years, vacuum containers have been set on top of each other so the tube is easily inserted from the top into the bottom container (see picture on page 76).

Advantages: It produces good coffee, full of aroma, clean and clear. This is an exciting brewing method, and following the process carefully is part of the ceremony.

Disadvantages: The timing is an important element and therefore, requires being closely watched during the brewing. Cleaning the brewer is difficult because of its large size and complex structure. Most vacuum brewing machines are made of glass which tends to break. These issues eventually caused the brewers to lose popularity.

MOKA POT (MACCHINETTA)

Moka pot brewer also known as stove pot coffee maker, moka pot or moka express is a simple and convenient coffee brewing machine, producing coffee that tastes very much like espresso. Because of its low price and good coffee quality, it has become very popular worldwide. In countries where coffee is part of the tradition such as Italy, moka pot brewers or Macchinetta (meaning "small  machine" in Italian) are found in almost every household. They are sold in coffee and accessory shops around the world. Collections of designer moka pot brewers have become a hobby among many coffee lovers. Although there are different types of moka pot brewers, either heated on a gas or electric stove, most are made of aluminum, stainless steel or glass.

At the beginning of the 20th century it was widely understood that to get good coffee, the water that passed through the coffee should not be boiled and the water pressure should be high to absorb maximum coffee oil that contains the aroma and taste components. (Today it's known the pressure should be about 9-10 bar). Before espresso machines were invented, the only device performing similarly was the moka pot brewer. With its octagonal aluminum container it was first introduced in 1933 in Italy by Alfonso Bialetti as Moka Express. Over the years it has seen great success and maintained its original shape.

How it works

The moka pot brewer includes three containers, the lower one for water, the middle one for ground coffee and the upper one for the brewed coffee. Heating the lower container creates pressure that pushes the water through the ground coffee into the upper container. The bubbling water shouldn't reach boiling point.

Beverage
Filter
Ground Coffee
Filter
Safety Valve
Hot Air
Beverage

How to use a moka pot:

1. Unscrew the moka pot brewer by separating the parts.
2. Remove the funnel and fill the bottom portion with water to the marked line. If there is no marked line, fill it below the pressure safety valve.
3. Insert the filter part and fill it with medium/fine ground coffee. Tamp the coffee to flatten the surface, but don't compress it.

④ Screw on the top container (it contains a rubber gasket that ensures the parts are sealed).

⑤ Place the pot on a medium stove burner and make sure the flame ring is smaller than the bottom of the brewer.

⑥ After a few minutes, the water will begin to flow up through the grounds, filling the top portion of the pot with coffee.

⑦ Turn the heating source off as soon as the flow stops.

⑧ Pour your coffee. You can also add some steamed milk to make a true Italian cappuccino.

A few tips for beginners:

- Moka pot brewers come in different sizes – for 1, 2, 3, 4, 6, 9 or more coffee cups. It's essential to use the exact amount of water and coffee for which it's designed.

- "Cups" mean espresso cup, 1oz (30 milliliter).

- Water escaping from the connection between the two parts may happen because the gasket is dry or the coffee is ground too finely.

- It's recommended to wash the moka pot (without soap) immediately after use and turn it upside down to air dry. In time the coffee-oil that coats the inside walls maintains the pot and improves the coffee taste.

- The filter and the gasket should be washed separately.

- Remember! The pressure safety valve is disposable. Once it bursts the moka pot brewer should be discarded because it's no longer usable.

- Do not use the handle to screw and unscrew the two halves of the moka pot brewer, it may break.

THE ESPRESSO WORLD

Espresso has become a very popular beverage in recent years and there are numerous good espresso machines on the market. This chapter is dedicated to espresso and espresso machines.

WHAT IS ESPRESSO?

Espresso is the beverage you get by running water at a temperature of 195°F (90°C) under pressure of 10 bar through ground coffee to extract as much as possible oils and taste components.

DEFINITION OF ESPRESSO

An attempt to define espresso was made by the (IENI - Italian Espresso National Institute Translated from *www.espressoitaliano.org*).

Italian espresso is prepared by running clear water at a temperature of 189-194°F (86-90°C) under a pressure of 8-10 bar through 0.25±10% oz. (7±0.5 gm) coffee ground to coarseness that requires extraction time of 22.5 to 27.5 sec. per cup containing 0.76±10% oz. (22.5±2.5 ml), at a temperature of 147-158°F (64-70°C).

The values in the definition of the American Coffee Organization are quite similar although the most significant difference is in the amount of coffee per cup 1.25 oz (38 ml). The preference of American or Italian style depends on individual tastes.

ESPRESSO MACHINES

There's a dispute regarding the source of the term "espresso." Some claim it stems from the word "express," but actually its origin is "expressly for you." Coffee brewed in an espresso machine is considered the best among the various methods. An espresso machine is the fastest way to extract the most oils and taste components from the coffee, which is the reason why so many people prefer espresso and why it attracts so many visitors to coffee shops around the world. In recent years more and more people have purchased domestic espresso machines in an attempt to achieve the same taste quality of the coffee served in their favorite coffee shop.

HISTORY OF ESPRESSO MACHINES

Many coffee shops were opened after the development of the coffee culture at the end of the 19th century. The need to serve a large amount of quality coffee in a short time motivated Luigi Bezzera, an Italian engineer,

Photo: Brevetto Bezzera's patent (1901), "Gigantic model"

to develop a coffee machine based on steam pressure, which he named Tipo Gigante. It was patented in November of 1901. The machine contained a sealed tank to heat the water and a faucet through which steam was poured over ground coffee in a metal filter for just a moment, quickly brewing the beverage.

In 1905 Desiderio Pavoni purchased Bezzera's patent and started producing espresso machines for coffee shops. The main breakthrough of espresso machines came in 1947 when Achilles Gaggia presented the first Crema Caffé machine that produced a high pressure of about 8-9 bar and had a manual piston with a temperature below boiling to make good espresso. These machines became very popular in coffee shops around the world.

Photo: One of the first model of Gigantic machine

ESPRESSO MACHINE TYPES

STEAM POWERED ESPRESSO MACHINES

Espresso machines without a pump are steam-powered machines. They contain a thermos-like container that heats water above boiling temperature and produces a pressure between 1.5-2 bar. When the steam valve is open, hot water flows through the ground coffee. The taste components extracted from the coffee create a beverage which is not espresso but something similar. These machines are inexpensive, they lack a pump, and the specifications indicate low pressure (2-4 bar) or do not indicate pressure at all.

Advantages: The machine is very cheap and easy to operate. It's more sustainable, provide continuous steam and there's no need to wait for steam to build.

Disadvantages: The beverage is not true espresso, but something similar.

MANUAL LEVER BASE ESPRESSO MACHINES

The lever espresso machine, also called a piston machine, is very beautiful. These machines often serve as decorative items. Very few companies still produce this type of machine for domestic use. Gaggia, Elektra and the most famous La-Pavoni offer a variety of elegant lever-based machines. La Pavoni is also one of the oldest companies that still produce espresso machines (it was established in 1945 in Milan, Italy).

Coffee connoisseurs claim that real espresso is produced only by lever-based machines. Brewing espresso by this method is difficult. Applying the correct pressure on the lever to produce good coffee requires a lot of experience. Pushing down on the lever produces the 9-10 bar suitable for preparing espresso, but maintaining a consistent pressure is not easy. Newer versions of the lever machine have a reversed system with a spring that applies force to the lever to create the correct pressure. The user pushes the lever down to fill the pressure container with hot water, and then let's go. The spring does the rest of the work.

Brewing coffee in a lever-based machine:

- Open the water tank cover, at the top of the machine, and fill the boiler.
- Close the water boiler cover and the steam valve. Push the handle down, plug in the machine and turn it on.
- Wait about 10 minutes until the pressure light turns off, or in machines with a pressure gauge, until the pressure is adequate.
- Insert freshly ground coffee into the portafilter (filter handle), tamp it, and return it to its place.
- Raise the lever handle slowly for about 4-6 seconds, until you hear the water entering the pressure cup. Wait 10 seconds to enable the water temperature to decrease to about 198°F (92°C).
- Lower the lever handle very slowly. The process should continue about 17-22 seconds. Watch the poured coffee and vary the pressure while lowering the lever to ensure a unified flow.

Caution: The machine body is very hot! When lowering the lever, it's natural to hold on to something with the other hand.
It's recommended to hold the machine at the base of the machine to avoid burning yourself.

Advantages: An experienced user can prepare an excellent espresso, the machine is very beautiful, and even if it's not in use, it can serve as a nostalgic, decorative item.

Disadvantages: The machine body is very hot, therefore it's difficult to add water while it's working. A training period and many failures are needed to achieve good results. The machine is covered with a shiny coating and every fingerprint shows. It's not built for serving large quantities.

SEMI-AUTOMATIC ESPRESSO MACHINES

 This machine, also called manual espresso machine, is the most domestic espresso machine in this category and is quite affordable. This machine type contains a cold water container, a boiler, pressure pump, control lights or a pressure control gauge, and switches. Water flows from the cold water container to the boiler, which heats the water to 194-203°F (90-95°C), The hot water is then forced through the ground coffee in the portafilter (filter basket). Most of these espresso machines contain only one boiler so it's necessary to use a switch to heat the water to boiling point to create enough steam to froth milk. The challenge in operating a Semi-Automatic espresso machine is to go from espresso brewing to milk frothing and back, because each step requires a different temperature.

Making coffee with a Semi-Automatic machine (single boiler)

It takes 14 steps to teach how to make the best espresso and cappuccino with a Semi-Automatic machine.

Italians claim that 4 "M" rules have to be fulfilled in order to make excellent espresso:

- **Macchina (Machine)** Only a good espresso machine that reaches the appropriate temperature and pressure enables extraction of the coffee oil that produces a quality beverage.
- **Macinatura (Grinding)** The grind coarseness (thickness) determines the water flow and the release of the taste components into the water (see Grinding, page 43).

- **Miscela (Blend)** The blend you use, its freshness and quality.
- **Mano (The man)** The operator of the espresso machine has to know how to prepare true espresso.

We believe there's a fifth requirement – but it doesn't begin with an "M" - the water quality. Water with a bad taste spoils the espresso (see Water Quality, page 103).

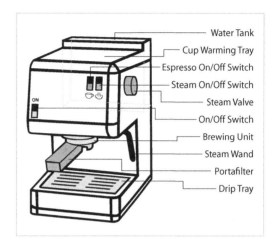

Water Tank
Cup Warming Tray
Espresso On/Off Switch
Steam On/Off Switch
Steam Valve
On/Off Switch
Brewing Unit
Steam Wand
Portafilter
Drip Tray

Preparing the machine:

Fill the container with filtered water without scale and switch on the machine.

Wait until the lamp signals the machine has heated up (5-15 minutes).

Espresso preparation stages:

Remove the portafilter and fill it with ground coffee. It's important to measure the exact required amount into the filter. Usually it's 2.5 oz (7 gr) for a single shot or 0.5 oz (14 gr) for a double shot.

Some professional portafilter baskets are larger and contain 0.3 oz (9 gr) ground coffee for a single shot or even as much as 0.37 oz. (10.5 gr). The double shot baskets are twice as big.

Compress the coffee with the tamper to flatten the surface, making sure to leave 1/16" (2 mm) space from the top of the filter.

Return the portafilter to its place and close securely.

⑥ Place the coffee cups under the portafilter. It's recommended to "prime" the cups with boiling water in order to maintain the ideal coffee temperature.

⑦ Turn on the pump – it's noisy when it's working. After about 5 seconds the coffee will begin to flow through the portafilter into the cups.

⑧ Let the coffee flow for 17-22 seconds (22-27 seconds after the pump begins working) or until the color of the flowing coffee turns to light yellow. The coffee flow from the machine is nicknamed "mouse tail" because of its shape. The thickness of the flow shows the flow speed and depends on the grind thickness.

⑨ Turn the pump off and serve the coffee.

Building steam – milk frothing

⑩ Turn the steam switch on for about one minute to enable the water in the container to reach the appropriate temperature – the lamp signals when the steam is ready.

⑪ Open the steam valve for about one or two seconds to release the water locked in the steam wand.

⑫ Froth the milk (see Milk Frothing, page 105).

⑬ Important – turn the steam building switch off!

⑭ Clean the steam spout with a wet cloth and open the steam valve slightly to clear it of milk residue.

If you wish to prepare another cup of espresso after frothing the milk, turn off the steam switch and wait until the water cools down before you restart espresso preparation (stage 3). The cooling process will occur faster if you open the steam valve and turn on the espresso switch for a few seconds.

Advantages: You can enjoy real espresso at home and the machine is relatively inexpensive.

Disadvantages: The machine contains only a single boiler, requires a long delay between preparing the coffee, frothing the milk and starting the next cup of espresso. You need to be experienced to get good espresso from the machine, and it creates dirt. There are espresso machines with a heating pipe instead of a boiler. In these machines, there's no need to wait to build steam (see Heating Methods in Espresso Machines, page 93).

FULL AUTOMATIC ESPRESSO MACHINES

This is actually the same espresso machine as the semi-automatic machines but with additional control system that stops automatically the brewing after a single or a double espresso dose.

SUPERAUTOMATIC ESPRESSO MACHINES

In the 1980s espresso machine manufacturers realized that customers were ready to pay more for convenience (or maybe for laziness), and the first superautomatic espresso machine was developed in 1991.

Since then the market for superautomatic machines has grown constantly. These machines produce "coffee-shop quality" coffee. The machine grinds the coffee to the appropriate coarseness, inserts the coffee into the proper filter, extracts the coffee, releases the debris into an interior garbage bin, and finally rinses itself so it's ready for the next cup. All this is done with the push of a button without any other human involvement.

These options are available in most superautomatic machines:

- A switch to adjust the grinding coarseness and a switch to determine the size of the coffee portion.
- A selector for single or double shot and the required amount of water – short or long espresso.
- Warning lamps when there's either not enough water in the water tank, or coffee beans in the grinder, and when the garbage bin is full.

Advanced machines contain additional functions that make the machine more expensive: two boilers, a digital screen, a larger tank for cold water, a direct connection to the water faucet, an option to use ground coffee, temperature controls, etc. In some machines an automatic milk frothing device is also included.

Advantages: It's very easy to operate and doesn't require specific skills. There is no need to continually watch the machine – it stops after the coffee is poured into the cups, occasional cleaning is simple and it's suitable for hosting because it can prepare an almost unlimited number of cups of coffee.

Disadvantages: It's expensive to purchase as well as maintain. It is usually made of plastic which can make it delicate and fragile, there's no manual control over the operation of the machine, and it's difficult to regulate when it's not adjusted.

CAPSULES AND PODS

To overcome some of the disadvantages of messy ground-coffee based machines, many companies produce small sealed packages of ground coffee for single espresso shots. The two methods are capsules and pods.

CAPSULES

The capsule is a small plastic or aluminum package of 0.175-0.28 oz (5-8 g) ground coffee, for a single espresso shot.

The capsules are either vacuum-packed or filled with nitrogen to prevent oxidation. Companies have an incentive to develop a unique capsule, usually patent protected, in order to create a captive customer base. To prepare the espresso shot, the machines punctures the capsule, and the pressurized hot water flows through the ground coffee to make the espresso.

PODS

A Pod is a small amount of ground coffee packed in a paper package similar to a tea bag. In 1998, Illy and several other leading coffee companies defined a new international standard pod they called E.S.E. (Easy Serving Espresso). The E.S.E contains 0.25 oz (7 g) of ground coffee and has a 1.77" (4.5 cm) diameter. This standard pod provides a simple solution for the customer who does not want to be committed to a specific manufacturer. Usually each pod is packed separately in a sealed foil package filled with nitrogen to prevent coffee oxidation. Once the package is opened, the pod begins to lose its freshness.

Pods vs. Capsules

Pods	Capsules
Freedom of choice: Freedom from being locked into a specific brand. Pods can be purchased in almost any coffee store with a number of flavor options.	**Being "married" to one company:** Capsules are available only from the machine brand and the flavors are limited (For a few popular capsules, competing companies produced compatible capsules).
Standard: Suitable for a variety of espresso machines. Many machines come with pod adaptors.	**Non Standard:** Suitable only for one brand's espresso machine.
Coffee source: The source is not always known. Some unqualified vendors produce and market pods with inferior taste, inadequate grinding, incorrect weight, etc.	**Coffee source:** The source is known. Quality coffee, appropriately ground with precise weight.
Less Expensive	**More Expensive**

Difference between ground coffee and pods/capsules

Ground Coffee	Pods	Capsules
Fresh	Undefined freshness, depends on when the ground coffee was packaged	
Messy	Clean	
Easy to prepare double espresso	Double espresso requires two pods or capsules	
Complex to operate	Easy to operate	
The user selects the coffee type	A large variety of coffee types	Limited variety, complete dependence on the espresso machine brand.
Price: Cheapest	**Price:** Less expensive	**Price:** Most expensive
Useful at home	Useful at home and office	

HEATING METHODS IN ESPRESSO MACHINE

The water heating system in an espresso machine is one of the most important features in determining the machine quality, coffee quality and machine durability. Espresso machines operate at two temperatures – low to produce espresso and high to produce steam. There are four water heating methods in espresso machines: heated pipe (Thermoblock), a heat exchanger and single or double boilers.

Heated Pipe - Water flows through a winding pipe wrapped with a heating element. In this method there's no need to wait for the water to heat – the machine is ready to use within a minute. Another part of the pipe is heated to increase the temperature above boiling point to create steam. Steam requires high pressure to froth milk. These machines use an internal pump to create pressure. A lot of water should be released before good steam is produced. The pump releases steam in pulses.

A Single Boiler - This is the most common water heating method in domestic espresso machines. In a single boiler the water is heated either to prepare espresso or to create steam, and the transition from one category to another requires a waiting period.

Espresso machine boiler

Heat Exchanger - This is the most common method in professional espresso machines, but it's also suitable for domestic machines. The heat exchanger maintains most of the heating advantages of two boilers without using a dual system. Therefore, they're a good option for the price.

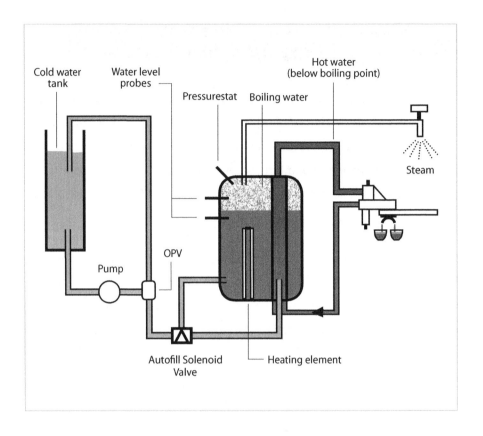

Cold water tank · Water level probes · Pressurestat · Boiling water · Hot water (below boiling point) · Steam · OPV · Pump · Autofill Solenoid Valve · Heating element

A tube is inserted into the larger boiler. The water in the outside boiler is heated to produce steam by a dipped regular heating element. The inside tube is heated by the water in the external boiler wrapped around it. A vibration or rotary pump creates the pressure to produce the perfect espresso. By this method espresso and steam can be produced simultaneously without limitation.

Two Boilers - This method is used by several professional machines. One boiler heats water to prepare espresso and the other produces steam and boiling water. Because of the amount of water in the boilers and the pace of their work, most of these machines have a fixed water inlet.

ADVANTAGES AND DISADVANTAGES OF HEATING METHODS IN ESPRESSO MACHINES

Method	Description	Advantages	Disadvantages
Heated pipe (thermoblock)	The water is heated during the preparation of the espresso in the pipe and not in a boiler.	The machine is ready to work immediately. Time to build steam is the shortest (very convenient in the morning when you're in a hurry). Enables continuous preparation of espresso shots. Perfect for espresso.	The water extraction temperature depends on the cold water in the water reservoir and the ambient temperature. The steam pressure is low, even though the pump is involved in the process. The steam is released in pulses. Not ideal for cappuccino and other beverages with frothed milk.
Single boiler	The most common method in domestic espresso machines. A single boiler with a heating element contains limited amount of water.	The water in the boiler heats fast (very convenient in the morning when you're in a hurry), very useful to prepare a small number of cups. Produces good quality coffee and the steam enables milk frothing. Small and stylish.	There's a prolonged delay between preparing espresso and releasing steam and vice versa. The amount of water in the boiler is small and the flow of cold water into the boiler during espresso preparation or milk frothing lowers the water temperature. It's impossible to prepare many cappuccino cups at once.
Heat exchanger	A small espresso boiler located within the steam boiler: The inner boiler has no heating source and is heated by the boiling water of the steam boiler surrounding it.	Frothing milk and espresso can be done simultaneously and produces almost unlimited number of cups.	The duration of water heating is relatively long in comparison to single boiler machines (depending on steam boiler size). Expensive.
Dual boilers	Each boiler is heated separately to the correct temperature and the milk frothing process is independent of espresso preparation.	Froths milk and prepares espresso simultaneously. Creates strong, stable steam which is excellent for frothing. Produces an unlimited number of cups.	Not eco-friendly, mainly because with two strong heating elements the electricity consumption is higher. More expensive.

Tip for espresso machine buyers

Higher pressure does not mean a better machine. Some companies boast high pressure – 18 or even 20 bar – as if it's a big advantage. For espresso brewing, no more than 10 bar of pressure is needed. Most of the professional machines produce pressure between 14 and 15 bar and include a special valve (OPV) that reduces the pressure to 9/10 bar on the coffee.

To find out which is the best espresso machine for you, see appendix page 203: coffee espresso machine buyer guide.

CREMA

You are sitting in a coffee shop or restaurant and you would like to drink a good espresso. How do you know if the espresso you've got is good? The common answer to this question is – take a sip and see.

Fortunately, one look at the espresso in the cup provides the answer, even before you taste it. One can learn a lot about espresso quality by its color and form. The brown copper-mahogany colored froth covering the espresso beverage is the "crema." It is created by the oils extracted from the ground coffee into the espresso beverage. When there's insufficient crema, the espresso is bad. However, good crema is not always an indication that the espresso is good.

The color of good crema is something between brown mahogany to copper and it will begin to dissipate after about two minutes.

The thickness of the crema on top of the espresso should be at least 0.04" (1 mm). It can easily be seen in a glass cup. Thick crema does not necessarily indicate better quality. Coffee blends rich in Robusta will produce a thicker layer of crema, but this will not always improve the coffee taste. Sometimes it indicates lower taste quality. Espresso without crema, or crema that dissipates within less than 20 seconds indicates that the espresso has not been prepared correctly.

| No Crema at All | Bad Crema | Watery Crema | Good Crema |

THE MAIN REASONS FOR POOR CREMA

- Coarsely ground coffee produces espresso without crema.
- If the amount of coffee inserted into the filter basket is less than necessary, you will get no crema.
- The crema will be whitish if the water temperature was too low.
- The crema will look like oily bubbles if the water temperature was too high, indicating the coffee was burnt.
- No crema or light crema can indicate that the coffee was not fresh.

There are other reasons, of course, – low coffee quality,
a faulty machine, etc.

CLEANING YOUR ESPRESSO MACHINE

There are two cleaning levels – daily and periodic cleaning.

DAILY CLEANING

To preserve the coffee taste and aroma, the machine should be cleaned twice every day – before using it and at the end of the day. The procedure is short but significant. To those who use it frequently during the day it's recommended you turn the espresso machine off only at night.

Morning cleaning

● Replace the water with fresh, cold water, insert the portafilter and turn the machine on.

● After about 10 seconds open the steam valve, activate the pump and let the water flow – about one quarter of a glass.

● Activate the pump as if you're preparing espresso for 10 seconds.

Cleaning in the evening or after the machine is turned off

● Empty coffee residue from the portafilter, remove the filter and clean it under water.

● Clean coffee residue from inside the machine group (the part connected to the portafilter) with a wet cloth or a suitable brush.

● Clean the area around the machine.

PERIODIC CLEANING
Backflush - Cleaning with a blind filter

Professional espresso machines with a 3-way solenoid valve (3-way pressure release valve) tend to collect coffee residue in the internal parts of the brewing system and in the pressure release tube. To clean it, use the blind filter (blank filter) to perform a "backflush."

This process should be repeated every two to three weeks (in a coffee shop it's performed on a daily basis).

● Replace the filter in the portafilter with the blind filter and a half teaspoon of cleaning detergent. It's recommended to use a special backflush detergent, not a regular home detergent, unless it's indicated explicitly by the manufacturer.

● Operate the machine for a maximum of 3-5 seconds as if preparing espresso. The residue and suds are released through the pressure release valve.

- Repeat the backflush until the water is clean without any remaining residue.
- Restore the regular filter and activate the machine for 30 seconds.
- Prepare two espresso shots with old coffee and check to see whether a soapy taste remains.

Three-way valve (3-way solenoid)

In each professional espresso machine, there is a three-way valve designed to release the accumulated pressure (10 bar) that remains in the portafilter, as soon as you stop the brewing process by turning off the water pump. On the other hand, in a basic espresso machine, that has no three-way valve, it is recommended to wait 10 seconds or more before opening the portafilter, or else the pent up pressure will spray the grounds all around.

Espresso State

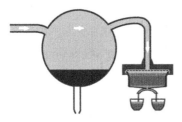

Position 1 - The three-way valve is in espresso mode - Hot water at 10 bar pressure flows through the valve to produce espresso.

Release State

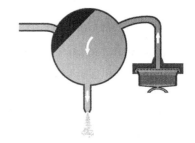

Position 2 - The three-way valve is in release mode - The accumulated pressure on the portafilter is released through the valve to the drain pipe.

DESCALING

Read the instructions carefully on the scale remover packaging and make sure it's non-toxic.

Espresso machines, like other water-heating equipment, tend to collect scale. To avoid machine damage, it's recommended to descale it thoroughly once every few months (timing of cleaning depends on the manufacturer's recommendation and your water quality). It should be done with a citric acid-based solution. Most espresso machine manufacturers supply cleaning material based on the type of machine.

Descaling may impair machine parts, therefore it's recommended to follow the manufacturer instructions. If the manufacturer doesn't supply cleaning instructions it's highly recommended to find out what materials were used for the boiler and heating element to avoid damage.

When no specific instructions are available, the common method to clean the scale in an espresso machine is:
(Not for machine with heat exchange or double boiler)

Use only a citric acid-based material for descaling (look for the small print or disclaimer describing the limitations of the material). Some use white vinegar as a dissolver, but it may leave an odor and a long leftover taste.

1. Disconnect the machine and let it cool for several hours.
2. Remove the cold water container and clean it thoroughly.
3. Dilute the descaling material with water, 1 teaspoon per 1 liter and pour it into the cold water container.
4. Activate the machine and release half a glass of water (~3 oz) through the espresso outlet.
5. Open the steam valve, activate the pump and fill a glass of water through the steam wand.
6. Close the steam valve and the pump and turn off the machine.
7. Leave the descaling material in the machine for about 10-15 minutes, or follow the manufacturer's recommendations
8. Repeat steps 4-7 three times or until the cold water reservoir is empty.
9. Remove the cold water container, wash it thoroughly and fill it with clean water.
10. Turn the machine on, open the steam valve, activate the pump and let water run through the steam wand until the container empties.
11. Add clean water continuously to the container. From time to time shut the steam valve for a few seconds and let the clean water flow through the coffee outlet.
12. Prepare a cup of coffee and taste it. If there's any residual taste repeat the washing procedure (steps 10 and 11).

WATER QUALITY

The main ingredient in coffee (98-99%) is water. Therefore, the quality of your water is very important. Often, tap water contains many important minerals for the body, but also significant amounts of calcium, iron, zinc, phosphorus and other substances that may have a negative effect on the taste, odor and clarity of your water. Chlorination to prevent water contamination affects both water and coffee taste. A water filter should be used to improve the quality.

SOFT & HARD WATER

Heated water leaves scale in kettles, espresso machine piping, dishwashers, etc. The rate of scale accumulation and its thickness depends on water hardness. The terms soft and hard water express the concentration of calcium (Ca) and magnesium (Mg) in the water.

Hardness can be divided into five levels depending on the concentration of calcium and magnesium it contains:

- Soft water – less the 3.5 Grain per Gallon – g.p.g. (20 mg/liter)
- Lightly hard water – 3.5-10 g.p.g. (20-60 mg/liter)
- Mild hard water – 10-20 g.p.g. (60-120 mg/liter)
- Hard water – 20-30 g.p.g. (120-180 mg/liter)
- Very hard water – more than 30 g.p.g. (>180 mg/liter)

Harder water causes a higher buildup of scale. Energy required for heating the same amount of water may increase by 40% as the result of accumulation of scale on the heating element. A softener can be used to reduce water hardness. The softener is a filter-like device that contains an ion-exchange resin.

Water Softener

The resin absorbs Ca and Mg. From time to time, when the softener is blocked it should be descaled with sodium chloride (NaCl) or with potassium chloride (KCl) (see Cleaning Espresso Machine – Descaling, page 101). The softener doesn't clean the water – there are special filters for this purpose.

A filter should be used to improve water quality and taste, and a softener should be used to prevent espresso machine scale. Some filters on the market are designed to perform both actions, but most are only filters and do not soften the water.

MILK FROTHING

Hot whipped milk is used in several types of coffee drinks such as cappuccino, café au lait, flat white, macchiato, etc. In some processes the milk is heated during the frothing and in others the milk is heated before frothing (It's not recommended to heat the milk after frothing because the froth might disappear).

Milk frothing methods are:

- Steam frothing by the espresso machine
- A dedicated frothing machine
- Spring blender
- Frothing container or a French press

Using espresso machines for frothing milk:

Streaming steam from the espresso machine steam wand through cold milk inserts small air bubbles in the milk causing it to heat and puff. You get smooth whipped milk, called microfoam.

- Hold an empty glass under the outlet and open the steam valve shortly to release the water trapped in the steam wand. Steam will follow a small amount of water flow. Close the valve.

- Pour the required amount of cold milk (3% fat or more is recommended), into the pitcher, preferably made of stainless steel, but do not fill more than half the pitcher.

- Immerse the steam wand into the milk and reopen the valve. Be careful! Opening the valve when the steam wand is not fully immersed in the milk may cause spraying.

④ Lower the pitcher until the wand tip is at the surface of the milk. The muffled noise indicates the milk is being frothed. If the steam wand creates big bubbles at the milk surface, lower the steam wand deeper into the milk. To create a circular movement of the milk in the pitcher, hold the pitcher at an angle.

⑤ As the milk expands the froth in the pitcher rises. Slowly lower the pitcher accordingly so the tip of the wand is always just submerged in the milk.

⑥ Steam the milk until it reaches the required temperature.

⑦ If the amount of foam is sufficient but the frothed milk has not yet reached the desired temperature, lower the steam wand deep into the milk jug to continue warming without frothing.

⑧ Even though milk's boiling point is around 212°F (100°C), heating milk above 155-158°F (68-70°C) will change its taste and texture.
A thermometer (see Accessories, page 110) or a hand on the pitcher will indicate when to stop the frothing process.

⑨ Clean the steaming wand with a wet cloth immediately after the frothing. Open the steam valve and release some steam to clear the inside of the wand of milk residue.

⑩ Tap the frothing pitcher gently on the counter to pop bubbles that have risen to the surface.

Steamed milk will separate into layers of froth on the top and hot milk below if left to stand for a few seconds. In order to produce latte art, a barista will continuously swirl the milk in the pitcher to prevent separation.

Advantages: The frothed milk is smooth with micro bubbles – microfoam – and is suitable for creating latte art.

Disadvantages: Frothing milk requires skill, the amount frothed in domestic machines is small, the steam pressure decreases quickly, it's impossible to prepare milk for more than two cups at a time, and the froth is not as thick as in professional coffee machines.

A Dedicated Electric Frothing Device

There are several dedicated devices to heat and froth milk. All you have to do is pour milk into the device, push the button and after a short time pour thick froth into your cup. These appliances should be cleaned thoroughly each time to avoid a sour milk taste. These devices are very convenient and are intended for office use.

Advantages: They're easy to use and produce froth quickly.

Disadvantages: They're expensive, consume space and if not cleaned promptly after use, produce an unpleasant sour smell.

Panarello

Frothing milk with a steam wand can be very frustrating. The panarello is easy and convenient to use. It's a small supplement assembled onto the steam wand. It contains a small hole on its side through which air flows into

the milk making frothing much easier. Simply insert about 1/2" (1-1.2 cm) of the panarello into cold milk, open the steam valve and the work is done.

Advantages: It's inexpensive and easy to use.

Disadvantages: It must be cleaned thoroughly after each use to prevent sour milk odor. The froth will have larger bubbles than you can get from a professional coffee machine, and will be less creamy.

Cappuccinatore

Cappuccinatore is a milk frothing supplement for espresso machines. One end is connected to the steam wand and the other is inserted into the cold milk container. The steam flow creates suction (according to the Venturi Principle) drawing the milk up from the milk container  and at the same time heating and frothing the milk. It's suitable mainly for small offices. It's easy to operate and the amount of froth is adjustable. There are various types of cappuccinatores and all are based on suction. It's very important to flow water through the cappuccinatore after each use to flush milk residue from the wand and prevent blocking of the openings.

Advantages: It's easy to use.

Disadvantages: It's difficult to clean, produces only mild frothing and its temperature adjustment is tricky.

Spring Frothing Wand

The mobile, small and inexpensive spring frothing wand is operated by batteries. It enables easy and fast production of milk froth. Insert the disc to the bottom of a half glass of hot milk 155-158°F (68-70°C), turn it on and raise the spring disc to the milk's surface. The texture of the froth is nice and delicate.

Advantages: It's simple, easy to clean, not messy, and fairly cheap.

Disadvantages: It can only froth one cup at a time, needs hot milk that cools during the frothing process.

Froth Pitcher or French Press

The milk frothing pitcher is a container with a cover and a lever with one or two nets at one end and a handle at the other. It's French press-like and can be purchased in most kitchen shops. Simply pour in hot milk and pump up and down a few times to form a rich, creamy froth.

Advantages: It's easy to use, simple to clean, not messy and inexpensive.

Disadvantages: It requires some effort to operate. Frothing hot milk, cools during the process. If the pitcher is made of glass it can be heated in a microwave but on the other hand it can break.

ACCESSORIES

Coffee companies produce a wide variety of accessories to make the life of coffee lovers easier. Some of them are very convenient and efficient to use and some are made simply to make a profit.

Knock Box

The knock box is a container for coffee grounds left after preparing an espresso shot. In coffee shops a large knock box is kept in a drawer next to the espresso machine. The user removes the portafilter from the machine after preparing the espresso shot, and knocks it against the rod in the box to release the used coffee grounds. It's recommended to keep a knock box at home next to the coffee machine for convenience and for better hygiene, instead of throwing the waste into the sink.

Thermometers

The preferred temperature of milk during frothing is around 155°F (68°C). Experienced users sometimes rely on feeling, but using a thermometer is more effective and precise. In some coffee shops a thermometer is always attached to the frothing pitcher.

Stainless Steel Pitchers

Stainless steel milk frothing pitchers are durable, unbreakable, don't rust and are easy to clean. During the milk frothing process, touching the pitcher enables you to feel the milk temperature and stop the frothing at the right time. They're available in different sizes depending on how much milk you need to froth.

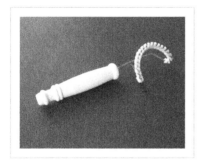

Cleaning Brush

The cleaning brush, used to clean residue from espresso machines group head. The brush should be strong and resistant to high temperatures. There's a large variety of cleaning brushes available. The picture shows a brush designed to clean the machine's O-ring seal in the group head.

Coffee Tamper

A round metal or plastic surface that fits the portafilter diameter is used to tamp the ground coffee. It's important to make sure the diameter of the tamper fits easily into the portafilter. In some machines, the tamper is fixed and attached to the grinder

and the tamping is done by lifting the portafilter up against the tamper.

Thermal Cups

It's a common sight – herds of people rushing to work, thermal cup in hand, enjoying the aroma and heat of their quality coffee on their way to work.

Portafilter Pod Adaptor

A pod adaptor, inserted into the portafilter (filter basket) enables the use of pods in espresso machines designed for ground coffee.

Cups

In addition to regular coffee cups, there's an abundance of collector cups all over the world. Coffee companies produce series of unique designer cups every year. The Illy Coffee Company, for example, produces an awesome collection of cups periodically.

Measuring Spoon

A precise measuring spoon, usually attached to every espresso machine, measures the exact amount for each coffee shot.

Cupper Spoon

Coffee cuppers in the world use a very flat spoon to taste coffee. The flat spoon, with a larger surface, releases more aroma which penetrates the cuppers' nose.

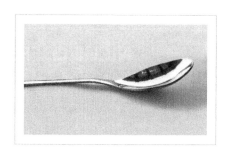

Blind Filter or Blank Filter

This is a special adaptor (a filter without holes) that corks the portafilter. The blind filter is used to clean espresso machines that have a 3-way solenoid valve (see Periodic Cleaning - Backflush, page 99).

Drawing Discs

These provide a beautiful way to serve coffee with a dusting of cocoa or chocolate powder shaped as a flower, heart, etc.

NICHE COFFEE MAKERS

If you were in the countryside with only a small fire and no source of electricity, you could still prepare a good cup of espresso.

In recent years, some new manually-operated espresso makers have appeared on the market that are capable of making good quality coffee. The high pressure produced by these devices is either manual or by fire.

Here are some of our favorites.

ROK

When the two handles are pressed down together they create the necessary pressure to produce quality espresso. Like in a regular espresso machine, coffee is placed in the portafilter, tamped, and hot water is added in the upper container. Then the two side-levers are lowered.

The water permeates the coffee at high pressure (8-10 bar).

Advantages: It's small, convenient, simple to operate and produces excellent espresso.

Disadvantages: The device itself is cold thereby cooling the coffee. It's recommended to warm it with hot water before use. It may require a few tries before making a perfect espresso.

Handpresso

The pressure in this device is produced by the hand pump, similar to a bicycle pump. According to the manufacturer the pump produces up to 16 bar (and contains a gauge showing the pressure).

Handpresso Operation:

1. Produce pressure with the pump until the needle in the gauge is in the green zone.
2. Pour 1-1.5 oz (30-50 milliliter) hot water into the reservoir.
3. Add ground coffee or a E.S.E. pod to the filter basket and close.
4. Turn the device upside down above the cup and press the release button.

Advantages: The device is small, portable, convenient, simple to operate and produces good espresso.

Disadvantages: It requires hot water and is limited to a single shot of espresso.

AeroPress®

Like a French press, but instead of the conventional metal filter, the AeroPress uses a plunger to force the coffee through a disposable paper filter, directly into the glass.

AeroPress Operation:

1. Remove the container bottom and place the disposable filter in the basket.

2. Wet the paper with a few drops of water.

3. Close the bottom and put the ground coffee into the container from the top.

4. Fill the container with hot water, stir and close the top with the plunger.

5. Wait shortly then press down on the plunger to release the clean, tasty and smooth coffee into the glass.

Advantages: It produces very clean coffee, it's lightweight, portable and convenient to use.

Disadvantages: It requires disposable paper filters (purchased separately). The device is not cheap even though it's made of plastic and unlike the French press, it allows preparation of only one cup of coffee at a time.

Bacchi

Imagine you're in the middle of nowhere with no source of electricity, but you're in the mood for a good espresso. Take out your Bacchi, fill it with water and ground coffee, put it on the fire and soon you'll be enjoying an excellent cup of espresso. By using water and fire, this small device can produce real espresso.

The Bacchi has two water chambers, one on top of the other. When the water in the lower container boils, it creates steam pressure which forces up a piston to create 9 bar pressure in the upper chamber. This forces the hot water in the upper chamber through the filter and the ground coffee.

Advantages: You get real espresso without using a pump, it's lightweight, portable and simple.

Disadvantages: It's expensive, you need to cool it before making the next espresso.

Vietnamese Coffee Maker

Vietnamese coffee (cà phê) is made with a coffee filter device which is used to prepare one cup at a time.

The device is a cylindrical metal container with a filter bottom. A second filter disk is inserted to tamp the coffee at the bottom of the container.

Vietnamese coffee preparation:

1. Place two teaspoons high roast (dark) coarsely ground coffee, into the coffee container. Shake the container to distribute the coffee evenly (some like to use Chicory instead of coffee).

2. Cover the coffee with the second filter and tamp.

3. Add one or two teaspoons of condensed milk into the empty cup.

4. Place the device over the cup and pour a dash of hot water into the vessel. Wait 10 seconds, let the ground coffee absorb the water and then pour in the rest of the hot water, filling the container.

5. Once the coffee stops dripping (about 4-6 minutes), remove the device.

6. Add sugar, stir and enjoy the taste of delicious coffee. There's also an iced coffee version (cà phê sữa đá or cà phê đá). Simply pour the drink into a tall glass filled with ice cubes and stir.

Percolator

The best definition for a percolator may be a hybrid between a moka pot and filtered coffee. The idea behind the percolator is a continuous drip of soaked coffee water over the ground coffee.

Some claim the idea of the percolator was invented by the British Benjamin Thompson.

The first "Coffee Percolator" patent was registered in 1865 by James Mason, but it wasn't the percolator we use today. However, in the U.S. in 1889, Hanson Goodrich registered the percolator patent as we know it.

Percolator structure and how it works:

The percolator is made of a tall water kettle with a coffee basket assembly inserted. The coffee basket assembly has a concave plate that collects the hot water at the bottom, and directs this hot water to rise through the central pipe until it sprays over the coffee basket filled with ground coffee at the top of the chamber. The hot water drips through the ground coffee in the coffee basket back to the bottom of the kettle, and then rises again through the central tube.

Ground Coffee

The longer the percolator percolates, the stronger the coffee will be.

COFFEE BEVERAGES

Hundreds of beverages are based on coffee. In many of them, coffee is only a pleasant supplement. Here's a compilation of many popular coffee-based beverages.

ESPRESSO TYPES

Short or Shot

Espresso basic shot of 0.25 oz (7 grams) of ground coffee approximately 0.85 to 1oz (25 to 30 ml) of beverage, produced in about 25 seconds (see Espresso, page 81). Served in a small cup. In some places it is called "short black," or just "espresso."

Long

Extended water on a basic shot of espresso 0.25 oz (7 grams) of ground coffee. The extraction time is extended to 45-55 seconds to get about 1.5-2 oz (45 to 60 ml) beverage. Also called Lungo.

Double

Two espresso shots 0.5 oz (14 grams) of ground coffee produces about 1.7-2.2 oz (50-65 ml) drink, called Doppio in Italian.

Quad

Four espresso shots (two double espressos).

Ristretto

A Very Intensive Short Espresso. Ristretto means "limited" in Italian. There are two ways to make ristretto. The first is to make a regular short espresso and stop the machine a few seconds (8-15) earlier than for regular short espresso. It's a very concentrated drink of approximately 0.5-0.85 oz (15 to 25 ml). The second method is to use finer ground coffee to obtain a smaller amount of potent drink, but it may damage the espresso machine.

Espresso Romano

Add a small piece of lemon peel to a short espresso and you have an Espresso Romano. The peel should be placed on the plate beside the espresso cup. Dropping the peel into the espresso breaks the coffee bitterness. This beverage can be found in many places around the world, but is less common in Italy.

COFFEE BASED BEVERAGES

There are several coffee beverages based on espresso and milk. Most of them are made with steamed milk. The way to prepare them can differ between each country or sometime even between cities. Below we refer to the common methods.

Cappuccino

This beverage combining one espresso shot with steamed and frothed milk became popular in the 1940s. According to legend, the name cappuccino refers to the Capuchin friars with their brown robe similar to the beverage color. The rules of the World Barista Championship state that cappuccino should contain  a harmonious balance between espresso, textured steamed milk and at least a half-inch of foam on the top decorated with a nice shape called latte art. It is served in an opaque cup of about 5-6 oz (150-180 ml). In a double cappuccino, double espresso is added. In some places cinnamon or chocolate powder are sprinkled over the top (see Latte Art, page 130).

Americano

This diluted drink is called Americano, made by pouring a single espresso shot into a 6-7 oz (180-210 ml) glass or cup and adding hot water. With the addition of some milk it tastes like an upgraded instant coffee.

Long Black

An espresso-based beverage made with hot water. Pour espresso over two-thirds a 6-7 oz (180-200ml) cup of hot water. Unlike an Americano coffee, where the hot water is poured over the espresso, in Long Black the espresso is poured over the hot water to preserve the crema.

Café Breve

Into a medium cup (4-5 oz 120-150ml), pour a short espresso and add hot steamed "half-half" milk or a mixture of equal parts light cream and milk. Compared to a cappuccino it has less milk but more fat.

Espresso Con Panne

A single or double espresso covered with whipped sweet cream is an Espresso Con Panna. Panna is Italian for "cream."

Macchiato

Macchiato means "spotted" in Italian and is made with a short espresso topped with one tablespoon of frothed milk to make a white blob on a brown background. Served in a small to medium 2.5-5 oz (70-150 ml) cup. There is also a double macchiato and long macchiato accordingly.

Latte

Latte means "milk" in Italian. This popular drink begins with a short or long espresso in a large cup, 6-8 oz (180-240ml) with hot milk or steamed milk topped with a thin layer of microfoam, no more then 0.4 in (1 cm) thick.

Latte Macchiato

The opposite of Macchiato – brown blob on a white background. Fill a small cappuccino cup 5-6 oz (150-180 ml) with hot whipped milk. Gently pour a single shot of short espresso through the middle of the froth, to create a nice brown splatter on top.

Piccolo Latte

Piccolo latte is in fact a small version of a cappuccino with less milk. The ratio between the milk and the coffee emphasizes the espresso flavor making the coffee more noticeable. Pour warm steamed milk over one shot of ristretto or espresso to a small glass cup 3-4 oz (90-120ml). The Piccolo latte is common in Australia and has recently spread to the rest of the world. In some regions in Spain the same drink is called Cortado.

Flat White

This coffee milk-based drink, common in Australia and New Zealand, has lately spread across the world. It's similar to latte, with a difference in the espresso to milk ratio. The Flat White has less milk and less milk foam. Sometimes it's served without any foam at all, but a little foam on top is recommended. Froth the milk slightly for a few seconds just to make the milk creamy. You can enjoy it hot or cold.

Hot Flat White preparation:

• One shot of espresso in a 5-6 oz (150-180 ml) glass or cup.

• 3/4 cup heated, creamy milk.

• 1 tablespoon of milk foam on top. The foam layer should be very thin, less than a quarter-inch (0.6 cm).

Cold Flat White preparation:

• Double or long espresso in a large glass (200 to 250 ml).

• Half cup of ice cubes, 3/4 cup cold milk and stir.

• 1 tablespoon of milk foam on top.

Layered coffee

Like an upgraded Latte Macchiato. Pour hot frothed milk into a tall glass. The milk will sink and the froth will float to the top. Slowly drizzle one espresso shot down along the inner side of the glass. Wait a few seconds to get three pretty coffee-colored layers.

Red Eye or Black Eye

If you need to keep awake and you need an extra caffeine shot you will probably ask for a "Red eye." Add to a cup of filtered coffee (French press can also be used) one shot of Italian espresso to get "Red eye," double espresso to get "Black eye." You can pour a small amount of milk on top and serve. This beverage is also called Hammerhead or Sledgehammer.

Café Au Lait

This is the most common coffee served in France. Pour a half-cup of filtered coffee (or French press) into 3-5 oz (100-150 ml) glass, and add hot milk. It's usually served at breakfast. Some coffee shops use long espresso instead of filtered coffee.

Wiener Mélange

The most popular coffee served in Austria is filtered coffee with cream or whipped cream and chocolate flakes sprinkled on top.

Iced Coffee

Enjoying fresh, iced coffee in the hot summer is a pleasure of coffee lovers. Fill 3/4 of a tall glass with crushed ice, add filtered or French press coffee and add milk or cream. For an extra special treat, add a scoop of ice cream or whipped cream and garnish with chocolate syrup.

Café Mocha

Coffee mixed with chocolate is called "mocha." Pour a double espresso into a tall glass, add three or four pieces of chocolate or two teaspoons of chocolate syrup or powder. Stir until the chocolate has melted and add hot milk. Sprinkle cocoa powder or chocolate chips on top.

Affogato

Affogato is an Italian dessert drink that contains the two elements that characterize the local kitchen, espresso and ice cream.

Place a nice scoop of ice cream, preferably vanilla, in a wide cup, pour over a shot of espresso or a double espresso for coffee lovers and add a tablespoon of amaretto. The coffee mixed with the melted ice cream and the amaretto is very tasty.

Granita (Espresso Granita)

There are many ways to prepare a frozen Granita. Here's one:

Prepare four shots of double espresso, add sugar as needed, 4 oz (120 ml) milk and the same amount of hot water. Stir well and let the mixture cool. Pour it into an ice cube tray and freeze it in the freezer.

Several hours later, crush with an ice crusher. Add 2 oz (60 ml) cold milk and pour into 4 tall glasses with whipped cream or a scoop of ice cream. Sprinkle with chocolate chips and serve with a long teaspoon.

Vanilla Cocoa

This light and refreshing summer drink begins with a double espresso, two teaspoons of cocoa powder and a half teaspoon of vanilla extract.

Pour into a tall, cold glass, add ice cubes and fill the glass with milk.

Cowboy Coffee (Also known as Campfire Coffee)

The western cowboys who led cattle herds to the other side of the country on a journey that lasted many months, used to sit around a campfire in the evening and coffee preparation was their main source of entertainment. Some claim that eggs were added to the water in the kettle (maybe that was how they cooked eggs), others claim residue from the previous coffee was used without washing out the coffee kettle because of lack of water or time.

Photo: Noa Cafri

While there are several versions of Cowboy Coffee, one popular version is: Place a cup of coarse ground coffee in a large saucepan with 8-10 cups cold water. Put the saucepan over the fire and stir from time to time. When the coffee starts to boil at the edges, remove it from the fire. Add cold water with a spoon, a spoonful at a time, and try to pour each spoonful in a different spot. The cold water sinks and pulls the coffee grounds down to the bottom. Wait four or five minutes and serve.

COFFEE AND ALCOHOL

Drinks that combine coffee and alcohol are popular in bars worldwide. The pleasant sensation of alcohol mixed with the stimulating effect of coffee is a great way to end an evening. Recipe books and the internet are full of recipes. Here are just two of the most famous alcohol/coffee drinks.

Irish Coffee

This is one of the most famous alcoholic coffee drinks. Irish coffee was invented by Joe Sheridan, a chef who worked at the Foynes airport in Ireland. At the beginning of transatlantic flights, planes were so small that nonstop flights were impossible. Even worse, the planes weren't insulated making it very cold during the flight. Ireland was one of the intermediate stop stations. Passengers had to wait while the planes were fueled. Irish Coffee was the appropriate solution for passengers looking for a drink that warmed and stimulated.

While there are many versions of Irish coffee, everyone agrees it should be served as a hot drink containing coffee, whiskey, sugar and cream or whipped cream. Whereas filtered coffee was used in the original version, espresso is very common today.

Preparation:

1. Whip heavy cream (stop before it thickens). Place in the refrigerator. Heat a large wine glass, 5-7 oz (150-200 ml) under a hot water stream from the espresso machine and dip it into a dish containing powdered sugar to create a light glaze around the glass rim.

2. Pour 1 oz (30 ml) whiskey into the glass and add a teaspoon of sugar.

3. Heat the whiskey for about 10 seconds with the steam wand of the espresso machine until the sugar dissolves.

4. The alcohol can be ignite (flambé) for impression.

5. Add a long espresso to the mixture.

6. Take the cream out of the refrigerator, hold a spoon upside down over the glass, pour the cream gently over the convex side of the spoon to drip slowly into the coffee. The cold cream floats to the top of the drink.

7. Serve quickly, while the cream is cold.

8. When sipping the drink, the unique blend of cold cream, hot alcohol, coffee and the sugar from the rim spreads in the mouth.

Coffee ala Liqueur

Mixing Irish Cream with coffee produces a rich texture and delicious taste.

Preparation:

1. Pour 1.5 oz (45 ml) of Irish Cream into a martini glass.

2. Add a long or double espresso.

3. Add one teaspoon of sugar (or substitutes).

4. Add frothed milk or whipped cream.

5. Sprinkle with chocolate flakes.

This is an amazing drink with a wonderful taste.

Any other liqueur can be used instead of Irish Cream.

SERVING COFFEE

Coffee is not just another drink, it's also a culture. Each nation has its own coffee culture and cultural experience. Like alcoholic drinks, each coffee beverage is served in a special cup and manner. For example, espresso cannot be served in a Middle East coffee cup and cappuccino cannot be served in a tea glass. Short espresso should be served in a small cup with a maximum content of 2 oz (60 ml).

Double espresso should be served in a medium half-filled cup, maximum 4 oz (120 ml). In many places espresso is served with cold water or soda-water alongside. Cappuccino is served in a 5-7 oz (150-210 ml) cup with nice latte art on top. You can decorate it with chocolate flakes, cinnamon

or cacao (see Latte Art, page 130). Bedouin coffee is served in a small porcelain cup without a handle. Middle Eastern coffee is served in half filled 3 to 4 oz (90-120 ml) glasses. Both Bedouin coffee and Middle Eastern coffee are served with sweet pastry.

It's a delight to receive a cup of cappuccino with a beautiful heart-shaped design on top, drawn by artistically pouring the milk foam into the cup.

There are three techniques that you can use to make a latte art: Free Pour, Etching and the Disk technique. In all techniques you should make a single or double espresso shot, and froth the milk to smooth well-frothed microfoam.

Free Pour Latte Art

Hold the cup with the espresso shot in one hand, tilt it slightly, and gently pour in the milk foam with the other hand. First pour from a height of 4"-6" (10-15 cm) above the espresso. After half filling the cup, bring the pitcher down close to the coffee surface (about 0.2"-0.5cm). By subtle wavy motions of the hand holding the pitcher and by varying the amount of microfoam poured, various images can be created.

Conventional designs include a heart, apple, leaf and rosetta.

For best results use a stainless steel pitcher with a narrow pointed spout.

Etching Latte Art

To create more complex shapes, you can use the Etching technique. In this technique you can use a toothpick or a special Latte Art pencil to draw a picture or even to write text on the white surface of the cappuccino.

Fill the cup with microfoam almost to the rim. You will get a white surface.

Dip the pencil through the microfoam into the depth of the coffee and then use it as a fountain pen to draw on the white microfoam with brown coffee "ink." It is almost the same way you would use a traditional pencil on white paper.

Disks Latte Art

In the disk technique you use disks, cut to different forms. Like in the Etching technique, fill the cup almost to the rim with white microfoam. Than place the disk over the cup, and sprinkle over cocoa powder, cinnamon or chocolate flakes (see Accessories, page 113).

COFFEE AND HEALTH

For hundreds of years, millions of people around the world have been enjoying coffee. Years ago, coffee was considered an unhealthy drink and many doctors recommended their patients to avoid drinking coffee. However increased health awareness in recent years, especially the popularity of natural products, has led to research on coffee to determine whether it's harmful or beneficial.

Despite the many studies, there's been no clear answer to this question until now and there are differences of opinion about coffee consumption. Although, there are still many who believe that coffee is not good for their health, it seems that coffee's image has changed to positive and coffee popularity has increased.

A large prospective study "Association of Coffee Drinking with Total and Cause-Specific Mortality" published in 2012 by the New England Journal of Medicine[1] claimed that coffee consumption was inversely associated with total and cause-specific mortality. The study found that, compared with people who did not drink coffee, people who drank 6 or more cups of coffee per day had a lower risk of death.

Other studies suggesting that coffee may reduce the risk of development of Parkinson's[2], dementia's[3] and possibly also Alzheimer's[4] diseases, but the evidence is inconclusive. Still further epidemiological studies do not provide a clear picture on the role of coffee intake in the development of hypertension."[5]

Coffee is comprised of a variety of components, the most famous and often disputed is caffeine. It's well known that caffeine has a stimulating effect and can produce wakefulness in many consumers. A caffeine overdose can lead to what is known as "caffeine intoxication." On the other hand, an abrupt cessation of drinking coffee may cause an unpleasant feeling due to shortage of caffeine in the body, and studies have shown that caffeine withdrawal causes symptoms similar to other addictive substances.[6] In these studies consumers kicking the habit showed symptoms that were grouped into 3 clusters: "fatigue and headache," "dysphoric mood," and "flu-like somatic."[7]

1. http://www.nejm.org/doi/full/10.1056/NEJMoa1112010
2. August 1, 2012, online issue of Neurology®, the medical journal of the American Academy of Neurology – Coffee may help some Parkinson's disease movement symptom
3. http://www.alzheimers.org.uk/site/scripts/news_article.php?newsID=1223
4. http://www.j-alz.com/node/168
5. http://www.ncbi.nlm.nih.gov/pmc/articles/PMC2605331/
6. http://www.ncbi.nlm.nih.gov/pubmed/15448977
7. http://www.ncbi.nlm.nih.gov/pubmed/18795265

Beside caffeine, coffee contains a large amount of antioxidants. It's now known that antioxidants protect the body against the development of chronic diseases.

Studies conducted on the effect of coffee on type 2 diabetes patients suggested that moderate consumption of coffee may be associated with reduced risk of developing type 2 diabetes. [8]

These associations still need to be clarified with more studies and research. Beware! Beverage such as tea, cola and other "energizing" drinks also contain caffeine (see Caffeine page 55).

Because of its stimulating effect, it's recommended not to overdo coffee consumption, especially for kids and women during pregnancy.

The Federal Department of Health of Canada recommends that pregnant woman shouldn't drink more than 300 mg of caffeine daily. [9]

They also recommend a maximum dose per day for children. [10]

Years	4-6	7-9	10-12	13 years and up
Maximum daily caffeine intake	45 mg	62.5 mg	85 mg	Child weigth (in lb) X 1.1mg Child weigth (in kg) X 2.5mg

In cases of uncertainty, it's recommended to consult a doctor or nutritionist.

8. http://www.coffeeandhealth.org/2013/11/14/moderate-coffee-consumption-may-reduce-risk-of-type-2-diabetes-by-25/
9. http://www.phac-aspc.gc.ca/hp-gs/know-savoir/caffeine-eng.php
10. http://healthycanadians.gc.ca/eating-nutrition/healthy-eating-saine-alimentation/drinks-boissons-eng.php

COMPETITIONS & CHAMPIONSHIPS

Awareness of coffee quality, increased demand for coffee and the spirit of competition have resulted in the development of international, annual championships for coffee professionals and fans, each year in a different country. The gatherings also feature some of the best coffee exhibitions as well as lectures by coffee experts from all over the world.

It's a real festival that enables coffee professionals and enthusiasts worldwide to meet, share knowledge and learn.

World Barista Championship

This is the most famous championship in the coffee world. The barista (Italian for "barman") is trained in the art of preparing and serving various espresso-based drinks in coffee shops. After a national competition, the winner represents his country in the World Barista Championship.

Competition rules:

Each candidate gets 15 minutes to prepare sets of: four short espresso shots, four cappuccinos and four cups of unique self-invented coffee beverages, all alcohol-free and without any edible material. The candidate's skills are judged by a team including a head judge, four sensory judges and two technical judges.

World Cupping Championship

This competition is to identify the best coffee cuppers. Each candidate receives eight sets, each containing three filter coffee cups (a total of 24 cups). In each set two cups of coffee are identical and one is different. The challenge is to identify the different cup.

The winner is the one who identifies more "different" cups. In case of a tie, the one with the fastest time wins.

World Latte Art Championship

The main goal in this competition is to test candidate talent and skills in preparing unique and beautiful shapes on the coffee surface with whipped milk (latte art).

World Cezve/Ibrik Championship

This competition takes place to select the best preparation of Middle Eastern (Turkish) coffee. Each candidate gets 12 minutes to prepare two traditional cups, two cups of hot special drinks in which the main ingredient must be Middle Eastern coffee and two unique cold cups.

World Brewers Cup

In this championship contestants compete on the preparation of the perfect cup of coffee (not Turkish coffee or espresso). Judges grade the quality of the drink: coffee to water ratio, coffee temperature,

taste (aroma, flavor, acidity, body, balance, aftertaste, etc.) and the candidate's serving and presentation skills.

World Coffee in Good Spirits

In this competition baristas' skills in preparing and serving alcoholic coffee drink are graded. In many places in the world alcoholic coffee drinks are common (see Irish Coffee, page 127).

World Coffee Roasting Championship

In this championship contestants compete on their ability to roast the perfect coffee. They use green coffee to prepare the best possible blend. This is a relatively new competition.

Most of the competitions are organized by the World Coffee Events (WCE) group, established under the auspices of two major coffee organizations: SCAA and SCAE.

To read about all competitions go to:
http://www.worldcoffeeevents.org/

REFUTING PREJUDICE ABOUT COFFEE

Following are facts that may change what you believe to be true about coffee.

Myth or Truth?

● **Boiled water should be used to prepare coffee, especially Middle Eastern coffee**

Myth: Coffee heated above 205°F (96°C) will have a burnt taste. Therefore, the Ibrik should be removed from the heating source before the coffee boils, or boiled water should be cooled slightly before it's poured over ground coffee in a French press or other coffee makers. The recommended temperature for good coffee is around 200°F (92°C).

Boiled milk should be used for cappuccino

Myth: Any coffee shop barista is acquainted with the phenomenon of people returning their cappuccino, complaining that it's cold. Even though the milk's boiling point is around 212°F, (100°C), overheating the milk changes its taste and texture. To get the best cappuccino, skilled barista heat the milk to around 160°F (72°C).

A thermometer (see accessories, page 110) or touching the pitcher will tell you when to stop heating.

Espresso machine with higher pressure pump is better

Myth: Recently, some espresso machine companies began to advertise their machines, emphasizing the high pressure pump, as if it's an important feature. However, pressure higher than 10 bar does not improve the coffee quality. Most of the professional espresso machines have a special valve (OPV – Over Pressure Valve) that releases pressure over 10 bar.

A high pressure pump in a thermoblock systems improves the steam whipping quality for milk frothing.

Instant coffee contains less caffeine than espresso

Not necessarily: One teaspoon of instant coffee contains between 60-120 mg caffeine, whereas an espresso cup contains between 60-160 mg.

Espresso containing 100% Arabica is better

You decide: Quite frequently coffee shop banners announce that their coffee is pure Arabica, indicating that they use better quality coffee. Not necessarily. Italians, for example, believe that each espresso blend should contain a certain percentage of Robusta, to diversify the coffee taste.

Arabica is always better than Robusta

Myth: About 65% of the coffee supply in the world is Arabica, much of which is of low quality. There is high quality Robusta that is much better than low quality Arabica.

Ground coffee can be kept in a sealed container for months

Myth: Ground coffee loses its characteristics rapidly. Coffee stored in an open container is inappropriate for use the next day. Ground coffee can be stored in a sealed container in a cold place for no longer than one week and even then it loses a major part of its aroma.

The longer beans are roasted, the better the coffee

Myth: The phrase that there's no accounting for taste is valid here. Some people like over-roasted coffee, but most people prefer coffee that preserves its taste and aroma.

COFFEE READING

Take a cup of black coffee, sip it noisily and patiently.
Cover the cup with a saucer and turn it over very carefully.
Glance intensively into the cup, what do you see?
A sunny future will emerge, or places you may get to be.

Reading in coffee has been known for hundreds of years. It's not scientific and there are no "facts" to point at, but there are principles in consensus. There are many methods to decipher the future in coffee. Here we attempted to offer some common principles. However, not everyone agrees with these methods. Reading in coffee reveals not only the future but also the present and the past.

PREPARATIONS

Prepare one or two cups of strong Turkish coffee in an Ibrik, and while cooking add the amount of sugar required by the consumer. When the coffee is about to boil and the bubbling gets closer to the center, remove the Ibrik, stir and return to the heating source. Do this three times. Pour the coffee into a small cup, preferably of white porcelain with a handle (the handle is important). Put it on a white saucer and wait patiently while the consumer finishes his drink. It's important to sip only from one side of the cup and therefore the cup should be held with the same hand the entire time. Do not attempt to push or guide. Let him drink quietly and wait until he finishes. Only the dregs should remain in the cup. Ask him to cover the cup with the saucer, close his eyes and silently wish for something. Then he should raise the cup and saucer together and turn them over clockwise three times, so the cup will be once upward and then downward, ending with the cup upside down on the saucer.

Now, wait a few minutes until the cup is cold. Do not talk to the client about work, love, family, etc., but discuss only general subjects, such as politics, or the weather.

READING IN COFFEE

The symbols or shapes that appear in the dregs that have been dispersed round the cup are clues to the consumers present, past and future. Symbols that are closer to the edge of the cup refer to the future and those close to the bottom refer to the past. The handle symbolizes the client – symbols appearing on the right side of the handle (clockwise) are positive  and on the left side of the handle are negative. Shapes close to the handle relate to something close to the client. Shapes such as an arrow, face, finger, etc., facing the handle are more closely related to the client's future and vice versa. A shape should not be interpreted individually, it should be viewed as part of a whole, because there's a connection between each shape and its adjacent shapes. The nature of each shape is also important, whether it's clear, blurred, overturned, part of a shape, etc.

KNOWN SYMBOLS

First, it's important to understand how to interpret a shape. For example, a circle may represent a ball, wedding ring, moon, etc., or it may mean that something is rolling toward you. Small lines around the circle may indicate the sun (strength, etc.). Therefore, it's important to observe what's in or around a circle.

Take a moment and look at the bold symbols, find the connection and then begin;

An arrow pointing at the handle: brings something

An arrow turned away from the handle: takes something away

Heart: love

Key: opportunity

Gate: potential success

Hand: friendship

Eye: jealousy

Demon: danger

Chain: bond

Ant: work

Knife: danger

Ear: news

Awl: gossip

Scissors: slicing, argument

Spider: unexpected money

Bee: may be friends, sweetness or stinginess

Spider web: someone trying to get ahold of the client

Full moon: date

Half a moon: something will happen in the middle of a month

Experience reading coffee yourself and enjoy!

COFFEE (KOPI) LUWAK

It's impossible to discuss coffee without bringing up one of the weirdest types of coffee called Luwak or Kopi Luwak, which is the most expensive and considered the best in the world. In south Asia, especially in Indonesia, the Asian palm civet,

Picture by Troy Davis www.animalcoffee.com

locally called the luwak is a coffee fruit-loving animal which roams around coffee plantations. The very greedy civet lives on fruits and eggs, but during the coffee season it's very fond of coffee berries and eats the ripened beans.

The natives collect the civet dry feces and send them to a processing center that collects the feces, determines they're authenticity, and separate the beans from the dung. The percent of humidity in the beans that are still covered with the papery parchment is high. The beans are dried on platforms in the sun for about a week. During this time the beans shrink and the parchment becomes dry, brittle and easy to peel.

Picture by Troy Davis www.animalcoffee.com

The beans are then sorted and marketed. The production of luwak coffee is very small. To supply the high demand, farmers started to raise the civet in coops and feed them with coffee fruit. Still, the demand is greater than the supply.

DID YOU KNOW?...

TRUE FACTS ABOUT COFFEE

- Many pain killing medications include caffeine.
- Most people decide on coffee quality by their sense of smell.
- A caffeine-free coffee replacement called chicory was popular in the 1950s.
- Filter coffee contains less than 1% fat, whereas espresso contains 2.5% and more.
- Coffee grows well on humus (leafy soil) and other organic material or on crumbled volcanic soil.

- In some places, smoke from burning straw is used to protect coffee plantations under extreme cold conditions. The heavy smoke adds a smoky taste to the coffee at the same time.
- The weather in Italy isn't conducive to coffee cultivation, but Italy is still a large coffee exporter. The Italians buy coffee and the blends they produce are sold all over the world.
- The Italians, one of the greatest coffee consumers in the world, like a very deep roasting, therefore a dark roast is called "Italian roast."
- In Turkey and Greece it's customary to serve coffee first to the elderly.

- The rumor has it the French philosopher Voltaire, was addicted to coffee and drank about 30 cups a day.
- Leftover coffee grounds can be used to fertilize the garden.
- There's a belief in Japan that bathing in coffee and pineapple improves the skin texture and reduces wrinkles.
- In some places in Africa, green coffee beans are soaked in water with other spices and then chewed.
- Snails and slugs are repelled by the smell of coffee. Spreading coffee grounds in the garden will drive them away.
- A mixture of coffee and sugar in a vase will bring back the color to flowers.
- Coffee is one the best odor neutralizers. In perfume shops, coffee is smelled to neutralize the previous perfume's odor.
- To produce flavored coffee, roasters add various syrups to flavor the beans at the end of the roasting process when the beans have good absorption, at about 105°F (40°C).
- A big increase in U.S. coffee consumption occurred in 1773. The taxes on tea were high and at the same time there were no taxes on coffee at all. This also led to the Boston Tea Party protest.
- Hawaii and Puerto Rico are the only places in the U.S. that grow coffee.
- Both, the French and the American revolutions were planned in coffee shops.
- Coffee became popular in Islamic countries because of the alcohol ban.
- In the year 1615 coffee was sold in pharmacies as a medicine.
- In December 2001 a coffee postal stamp with the scent of coffee was introduced in Brazil. The smell lasted about 3 years.
- Despite progress, coffee picking is mostly done manually by exploited workers.

- Some say a woman in Turkey could demand a divorce from her husband by claiming that he refused to give her coffee.
- About 5 million workers are engaged in coffee harvesting and processing in Brazil.
- Cappuccino is named after the Capuchin friars. Some say this is because of their brown clothing.
- 30 lb (14 kg) red coffee cherries produce about 5 lb (2.3 kg) of roasted coffee beans.
- Seasonal harvest of one coffee tree yields 7-12 lbs (3-5.5 kg) of coffee cherries.
- Drinking 3 cups of coffee daily per year is the yield of 15 coffee trees.
- On average, 1 lb is about 2,700 beans (1 kg contains about 6,000 beans).
- An average of 42 coffee beans is needed for one espresso shot, 0.25 oz (7 gram) of ground coffee.

FREQUENTLY ASKED QUESTIONS (FAQ)

The following questions are frequently asked in various coffee forums:

- **Which espresso machine should I buy?**

  This is the most common question and there's no definitive answer. It's like asking what car or camera to buy. There are dozens of espresso machine types, different prices and different qualities.

  Our recommendation is to read the chapter on espresso machines and then consult our decision tree to understand which machine is best for you. Use the questionnaire (page 206) to select the appropriate machine. Buy it in a store that specializes in espresso machines, where you can receive good advice, a demonstration and long-term service.

- **Why does the coffee in my espresso machine flow too fast?**

  It may happen either because the coffee is ground too coarsely or the amount of coffee in the portafilter basket is low.

- **Why does the coffee in my espresso machine drip or trickle slowly?**

  It may be because the coffee is ground too finely or there is too much coffee in the portafilter basket. It could also be because the machine is full of scale and needs descaling, or a pump problem.

- **Why is there no crema on my espresso?**

  It could be because the coffee flows too fast, water temperature is off, the coffee is old or the machine is not producing enough pressure.

- **What affects the taste and quality of the coffee we drink?**

  Aside from the preparation method, the equipment quality and the level of skill of the preparer, here are the major factors that affect coffee taste and quality:

• Coffee tree type (Robusta, Arabica)
• Growing region
• Processing method (washed or unwashed)
• Bean freshness
• Roasting level
• Water quality and temperature
• Proper grinding
• Ground coffee-water ratio

● Do the various coffee processing methods (unwashed versus washed) create differences in flavor?

Yes! Sometimes processing methods affect coffee flavor even more than its variety. In the unwashed (dry) process method the coffee cherries are spread on the ground in the sun for a long time, absorbing the shell flavor. Therefore their flavor is sweeter, smoother and with more body whereas the washed (wet) coffee has more acidity and less body. The quality obtained by the unwashed method is low compared to the washed method, but it's less expensive.

● How do you create several color layers in the coffee glass?

Layers are created with liquids of different density: coffee, milk and milk foam. Pouring the coffee gently into the glass over whipped hot milk creates the different layers.

A detailed description can be found in the chapter on Coffee Drinks.

● Is it necessary to warm coffee cups?

It's not necessary but recommended, especially before preparing espresso. Cold glass causes an immediate decrease in the coffee temperature.

● **How long should espresso extraction take?**

28 ± 5 seconds after turning on the pump, or about 23 ± 3 seconds after the coffee begins to run.

● **When making espresso, how hard should I press the tamper in the filter basket? Is it really necessary?**

Yes it's necessary! Tamping ground coffee allows the hot water to flow uniformly through the coffee, and creates the resistance to the pump pressure. How hard to press? Between 10-40 lb (5-20 kg).

● **What is caffeine and what is its flavor?**

Caffeine is a bitter substance found in plants and leaves. Warning! Large amounts of caffeine can cause caffeine intoxication (see Caffeine, page 55).

● **How much caffeine is in a cup of coffee?**

From 60-160 mg of caffeine in each cup of coffee, depending on the coffee variety and preparation method (see Caffeine, page 55).

● **I drank coffee in a restaurant and it was very sour. Why?**

Some restaurants use a drip system to prepare coffee. If they leave it in the glass carafe on a heating plate, the coffee begins to oxidize and becomes sour. You might want to wait until a fresh pot of coffee is prepared and then ask for your coffee.

● **I've had an espresso machine for months now. What should I use to descale it?**

The best descaling is done by the substance provided by the machine manufacturer. If it's not available, other commercial non-toxic cleaning substances for similar espresso machines can be used. If there's no other option, it's also possible to use one teaspoon of citric acid per liter of water as a descaling solution (see Descaling, page 101).

Do I need to tamp the coffee in the moka pot?

No, only fill the filter with ground coffee and level the surface.

I made coffee for two in a large moka pot and obtained a really weak coffee? Why?

There are several sizes of moka pots – single, two, three, four cups, etc. Every size has its suitable filter for an exact amount of coffee. If you insert less coffee, the coffee will be weak.

Is coffee an addictive drug?

Experts say it is. A common definition for a drug addict is a person who will do anything to get their drug. I've never heard of someone breaking into a coffee shop to get their coffee. In my opinion, coffee is not an addictive drug.

Is it healthy to drink coffee?

There are different opinions regarding coffee's effects on health. It's well known that coffee is stimulating. Many doctors say coffee is unhealthy, but on the other hand, many others claim it has positive qualities. If you have doubts, consult your doctor (see Coffee & Health, page 132).

How do I know if the coffee I buy is fresh?

An expiration date should appear on the package. Usually, it's one year from the roasting date, sometimes it's 18 months. In a vacuum package or sealed cans it can be even 2 years. But be aware that this is not the date when the coffee is not fresh any more, after that date it's not recommended to drink the coffee. If there is no date, and it's difficult to know if it's fresh, don't buy it.

What's the best way to store coffee?

A sealed bag or vacuum can and a dark, dry and cold place provide the best conditions for storing coffee (See ,Storing, page 51).

I heard that it's not recommended to put coffee beans in a sealed bag immediately after roasting. Is this true?

True. Coffee beans emit gas for about two or three days after roasting. Companies use bags with a one-way valve that emit gas but prevent penetration of air and moisture. You can also wait three or four days before sealing the bag.

What's the best grind for my espresso machine?

Appropriate grinding provides one espresso shot in 23 ± 3 seconds. Each machine requires a specific grind. Most coffee shops will provide the coarseness appropriate for your espresso machine or you can use the trial and error method to learn (see Grinding, page 43).

I heard that paper filters aren't healthy. Is it true?

In the past, paper filters were bleached by unhealthy methods that left a bad taste in the mouth. Today paper filters are bleached using oxygen, which prevents the bad taste and is harmless to people as well as the environment. There's also a brown paper filter that isn't bleached at all.

What's the best way to keep a coffee beverage fresh?

Cold coffee will stay fresh in the refrigerator and hot coffee in a thermos for several hours.

Is it healthier to drink decaffeinated coffee?

It depends on who you ask. Although the coffee is caffeine-free, there are some decaffeinating methods that use hazardous substances. Therefore the answer is not unequivocal (see Decaffeinated Coffee, page 61).

Why is there a difference in roasted coffee colors?

It depends on the type of coffee beans, roasting duration and method. Longer roasting time causes beans to turn darker (see Roasting, page 30).

COFFEE IN THE WORLD

Coffee grows in about 80 countries around the world. The yield of each country varies from one year to another and from one season to the next. Some countries grow the Arabica variety and others the Robusta. Some countries grow both (see Coffee Countries, page 158).

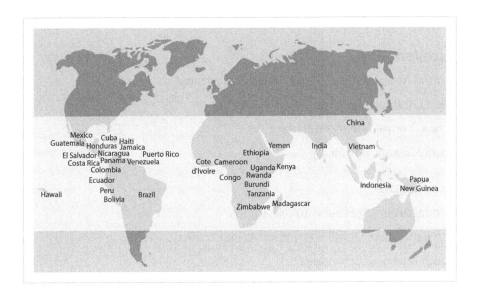

COFFEE RATING IN THE WORLD

It's very difficult to agree, which is the highest rated coffee in the world. Some believe "Blue Mountain" coffee from Jamaica is the best. It may be, yet it's not clear whether its taste justifies its high price. On the other hand, many people, especially those in the U.S., prefer Hawaiian "Kona" coffee, which they believe to be superior. It also happens to be very expensive. From time to time people will agree to pay quite a bit for a special coffee.

In 2013 a buyer paid $350.25 per pound for Panama "Esmeralda Special" coffee.

Coffee quality can be divided into four levels: excellent, very good, good and the others. Different countries produce different quality coffee. Here's a list of coffees graded by quality and country. It represents our opinion and may be graded differently by others.

Excellent
Central America: Costa Rica, Guatemala, Panama
The Caribbean: Jamaica
Africa: Kenya, Yemen, Ethiopia
Pacific Ocean: Hawaii

Very Good
Central America: El Salvador, Nicaragua
The Caribbean: Dominican Republic, Puerto Rico
South America: Colombia
Africa: Zimbabwe, Uganda (unstable)
Asia and Oceania: Java - Indonesia, Papua New Guinea

Good
Central America: Mexico
The Caribbean: Haiti, Brazil
South America: Ecuador, Venezuela
Africa: Tanzania
Asia and Oceania: Sumatra (Indonesia)

The grading changes every year and therefore the list refers to the data at the time this book was written. One bad year is enough to change the grading of a country. Also sometimes even "excellent" coffee can be spoiled by the time it reaches the end user.

COFFEE TASTE FEATURES - BY REGIONS

Coffee also can be divided, according to taste, into four main regions.

- Africa and the Arab countries
- South America
- Central America and the Caribbean
- Asia and the Pacific islands

Despite this division, the features of coffee grown in a certain region aren't necessarily similar. There are differences between plants in each country due to height, climate, soil type, cultivation methods, harvest, drying, etc. Coffee doesn't always follow the "regional rules" (e.g. coffee from Africa and the Arab countries is more acidic). Therefore, characterization of coffee in different places around the world relates only to its general features.

Africa and the Arab Countries

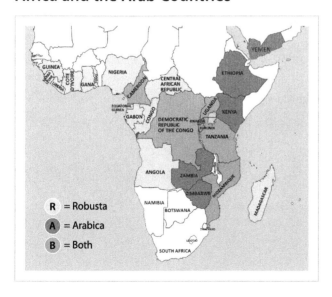

155

The taste of coffee from Arab countries is defined as the original coffee taste. It's characterized by high acidity with a slight fruit and chocolate flavor. With its good aroma and medium body, it's considered excellent coffee and is in high demand in the world. For example, the taste of Ethiopian coffee is well known for its unique taste with good acidity. Kenyan coffee is considered one of the most exotic in the world.

South America

About half the coffee marketed in the world is grown in this region. Brazil alone grows about 30% of the world consumption and Colombia is the third/fourth coffee producer in the world - about 6% of the global demand. The coffee grown in this region is balanced and suitable for many coffee blends. It's characterized by medium-weak body, and medium acidity and aroma. Other coffee growers in South America are Peru, Venezuela, Bolivia and Ecuador.

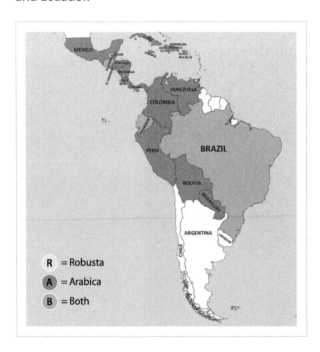

Central America and the Caribbean

Coffee from this region is highly valued, and is in high demand in the world, due to its exceptional quality. The main producers are: Jamaica, Haiti, Puerto Rico, the Dominican Republic in the Caribbean, and Costa Rica, Panama, Honduras, Nicaragua, Mexico and Guatemala in Central America. Coffee from the Caribbean islands and Central America is characterized by a strong aroma and its aftertaste remains in the mouth for a long time. Its acidity and body are medium, with perfect balance and good complexity, which is why it's used in blends with almost all other coffee varieties.

Asia, Indonesia and New Guinea

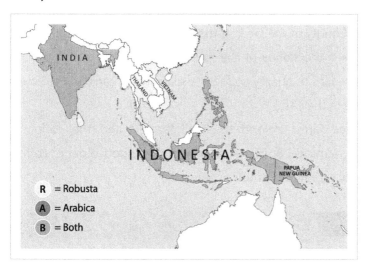

Indonesia, India and Vietnam are the world's main Robusta suppliers. They also produce some good quality Arabica. The coffee produced in this area usually have low acidity and a heavy body, expressed mainly by its viscosity that's similar to olive oil. The coffee taste is very special with a light grassy flavor.

COFFEE COUNTRIES

BOLIVIA

Surrounded by Argentina, Paraguay, Brazil, Peru and Chile, located the South American country of Bolivia. The capital La Paz, is situated on the huge ridge of the Andes at an altitude of 11,800 ft (3,600 m), and its coffee plantations are located lower at a height of 3,300-4,900 ft

Photo: Cohen Floch, Isla del Sol, Bolivia

(1,000-1,500 m). Most of the Bolivian coffee (90%) comes from the Yungas region in La-Paz County in the west of the country. The high humidity and copious rain makes the slopes of the Andes perfect for growing quality coffee. A small amount of quality coffee is also grown in Tarija in the south and in Santa Cruz in the east.

Since most coffee farms belong to small farmers and the coffee is grown without chemicals, Bolivia is known for its good organic coffee. Bolivia grows only varieties of Arabica.

About	Bolivia
Area	424,164 sq mi (1,098,581 km²)
Population	Over 10M
Taste	Bolivian quality coffee has a very strong aroma, medium body and its acidity remains in the mouth for a long time
Preferred roast	City to maximum Full-city
Washed or Unwashed	Mostly wet
Classification	By defect

BRAZIL

Brazil, the largest country in South America, is also the largest coffee producer in the world, providing about one-third of the world's consumption. The vast coffee growing areas are located on small farms nestled on the mountain slopes. The main crop grown in Brazil is Arabica, but it also produces Robusta. Both are processed by the dry method, under superb weather conditions. During the drying process the coffee taste gains some of the peel sweetness that penetrates the beans, reducing their acidity.

The average quality of Brazilian coffee is considered low, but the country also produces expensive quality coffee. When one announces that he uses Brazilian coffee, without further details such as brand or classification, it usually means he uses cheap coffee of poor quality with no grade. Because of the large amounts and low production costs, most of the Brazilian produce is directed to the coffee industry. Recently, Brazilian coffee organizations have invested significant efforts to improve the world image of Brazilian coffee. Those groups are aiming to produce high quality Brazilian estate coffee.

Photo: Mechanical coffee picking,
Nossa Senhora Aparecida farm, Brazil - Dallis Bros.

Most of the Brazilian coffee produces in the west part of the country. More than 50% of Brazilian coffee is produces in the Minas Gerais region in Southwestern Brazil, most of it Arabica. The state of Espirito Santo is the second largest coffee producer, most of it Robusta. Known quality coffee species from Brazil are Bourbon Santos and Bahia.

In September 2003, the Brazilian government found 600 slaves on a coffee farm in Bahia. Discovery of slavery in the twenty-first century created an international furor and has brought about a positive change in employment conditions in coffee plants plantations.

Gourmet Brazilian coffee is used mostly for espresso blends but it's also good for espresso as a single origin.

Photo: Harvesting Coffee, Alto Cafezal Estates, Patrocínio, Minas Gerais, Brazil

About	Brazil
Area	3,287,612 sq mi (8,514,877 km^2)
Population	205M
Taste	Because of the large amounts of coffee produced in this country, there's a wide range of coffee flavors. Generally, we can characterize Brazilian taste is sweeter and less acidic than other Central American coffees.
Preferred roast	Roasting for most Brazilian coffee varieties is City to Full-city
Washed or Unwashed	Unwashed and washed (also semi-washed)
Classification	By defects, taste, screening size and region of growth

BURUNDI (Republic of Burundi)

The small mid-African country of Burundi, bordered by Rwanda, Tanzania and The Democratic Republic of the Congo, produces quality Arabica coffee. A few years ago Burundi was one of the 25 largest coffee producers in the world, but in recent years its production has decreased.

Burundi is located in highlands. Its lowest point at Lake Tanganyika is 2,500 ft (760 m) and its highest is the adjacent Mount Heha at 8,760 ft (2,670 m). Most of the coffee plantations are spread in the western and central parts of the country at altitudes between 3,600 and 6,250 ft (1,100-1,900 m). Eighty-five percent of the population make their living from agriculture, coffee being one of the main crops and a significant source of foreign currency due to the high price in the market for quality Burundi coffee. For their own consumption locals use low grade coffee. The farmers pick the cherries and send them to SOGESTAL (Societe de

Gestion des Station de Lavage), coffee-washing stations that buy beans from growers across Burundi. The green beans are then sent to dry at milling stations (currently there are eight in Burundi). After drying, sorting and grading they are stored in warehouses of the Coffee Board of Burundi (OCIBU).

Photo: SuSanA Secretariat & Richard Kaderi

About	Burundi
Area	10,745 sq mi (27,830 km^2)
Population	10.5M
Taste	Burundi coffee is clean with strong body, balanced with good acidity and aroma, and a slight sweetness and a shade of chocolate in the background. Its features are similar to the wild African coffee, but with less acidity.
Preferred roast	The recommended roasting is City
Washed or Unwashed	Mostly washed
Classification	A combination of defects and screen + process method

CAMEROON

Located on the Gulf of Guinea in West Africa, Cameroon is considered one of the more stable and progressive economies among the surrounding western African countries. Even though the main agricultural produce of Cameroon is cocoa, coffee provides a significant part of the national income.

Cameroon's annual coffee production is around 500,000 bags (ranked 17-20 in the world).

The majority of Cameroon's production is Robusta (dry and washed). Between 10-

Photo: Bill Zimmerman, Coffee seedling & fresh beans

15% of the production is good quality washed Arabica, that was brought to Cameroon by the Germans at the beginning of the 20th century. The Arabica grows in the North West of the country in the Foumban region, in small farms, while most of the Robusta is grown in the South and South West around the Littoral region and East of the capital Yaounde. Cameroon coffee is exported to Europe, mainly to Italy.

About	Cameroon
Area	183,568 sq mi (475,440 km^2)
Population	20M
Taste	Quality Arabica coffee – contains high acidity, medium body and good aroma
Preferred roast	Full-city
Washed or Unwashed	Both washed and unwashed
Classification	By screen, size, defects and process

COLOMBIA

This northern South American country is ranked in the top three to four coffee producers in the world, after Brazil and Vietnam, and its produce is similar to that of Indonesia.

Photo: Oscar E. Monsalve - Colombia

Coffee is grown in west Colombia on the slopes of the Andes that runs from north to south. The temperature at the coffee plantations is stable due to Colombia's proximity to the equator. The best known Colombian brands are Medellin, Armenia, Manizales, Bogota and Bucaramanga.

Many coffee lovers would recognize the picture of the mustached Juan Valdez leading his donkey through the Colombian coffee fields, but only a few know that he was actually a famous South American actor. This logo was created in 1959 to present worldwide, the hard work and the dedication behind Colombian coffee.

Café de Colombia
www.JuanValdez.com

One of the largest non-profit coffee organizations in the world – the coffee growers' federation (FNC – Federación Nacional de Cafeteros) in Colombia, was established in 1927. With more than half a million coffee farmers, much effort has been invested by the Colombian government in supervising and improving the coffee quality. Only high graded coffee can be exported. The outcome was an increase in its popularity in Europe and in the national income. Another reason for the popularity of Colombian coffee is that the coffee is produced all year long.

However, most of the Colombian coffee is harvested manually and the almost slavery living conditions of the working families are inexcusable. In recent years the Colombian government tried to put an end to the mistreatment of children employed in coffee plantations.

About	Colombia
Area	439,735 sq mi (1,138,910 km²)
Population	45M
Taste	Its good aroma, rich fragrance, medium heavy body and delicate acidity are known all over the world
Preferred roast	Can be roasted to various levels, but the recommended roasting is between City to Full-city
Washed or Unwashed	Washed
Classification	By screen size and defects (large beans are called Supremo and small ones Excelso)

THE DEMOCRATIC REPUBLIC OF THE CONGO

The civil war between the tribes that began in 1994 ripped apart the landlocked central African country (previously Zaire, Belgian Congo or Congo Kinshasa). More than 73 million citizens in the country suffer from poverty, diseases and conditions of poor sanitation. Only a small part of their good quality coffee is exported. Most of their production is for domestic consumption. Because of the war, the coffee production decreased and its quality deteriorated. A few hundred farmers in small villages make their

living from coffee farming, using the unwashed method. Despite the good conditions, 80% of the Robusta processed by the unwashed method is inferior. Higher quality Arabica is grown in the Kivu region in the eastern heights bordering with Tanzania, Rwanda and Uganda.

About	The Democratic Republic of the Congo
Area	905,355 sq mi (2,344,858 km²)
Population	73M
Taste	High quality Congo coffee has clear acidity, its aroma is strong with fruit and vanilla in the background
Preferred roast	Full-city to French dark roast and should be used after waiting at least for three days, otherwise it will contain a shade of a rubbery taste
Washed or Unwashed	Washed and semi-washed
Classification	By defects

Photo: The LEAF Project, Modern Languages @ FLCC - Costa Rica

COSTA RICA

The small Central American country of Costa Rica produces about 1.5 million bags of coffee each year. Its coffee is considered among the best in the world, and is in high demand worldwide, especially in the U.S. Coffee from Costa Rica is described as romantic and exotic.

Many coffee lovers drink it as a single origin and not in blends.

By government law Costa Rican farmers are permitted to plant only Arabica trees and the majority of their coffee is defined as "gourmet." Most of their coffee grows in two Costa Rican mountainous areas: one is Tres Rios, close to the shore and the capital of San Jose, and the other is Tarrazu, located in the inner mountainous part of the country.

Photo: The LEAF Project, Modern Languages @ FLCC - Costa Rica

Costa Rican coffee brand names refer to the district they come from or their variety. The quality coffee brand names: San Marcos di Tarrazu, Heredia, Alajuela, Bella Vista, La Magnolia, El Legendario, Dota (also called Dota Tarrazu or in its commercial name Dota Conquistador) and La Minita, are considered the best among the quality coffee brands. Coffee from these regions is mild and fruity.

About	Costa Rica
Area	19,730 sq mi (51,100 km²)
Population	4.6M
Taste	Costa Rican coffee is characterized by heavy body, strong aroma, and medium to high acidity, amazing smoothness and nice aftertaste that lingers in the mouth
Preferred roast	Roasted to City for espresso
Washed or Unwashed	Washed
Classification	By altitude and region/estate

THE DOMINICAN REPUBLIC (DR)

The conditions for growing coffee in the Dominican Republic, on the Hispaniola Island in the Caribbean, are ideal. Most of the DR coffee is grown on the slopes of three Mountain ranges in the north, the highest mountain Pico Duarte 10,420 ft (3,175 m), the center one and in the east of the country. The DR produces six well-known coffee brands: Cibao, Bani, Ocoa, Azua, Barahona and Juncalito. Barahona and Juncalito are valued as the best coffee brands in the country and are therefore difficult to obtain. The beans' shape and taste are different than other brands.

DR coffee bag

This type of coffee is very similar to other Caribbean coffee brands and can be used as a single origin or blended with other varieties to obtain wide-ranging types of coffee. A picture and the name "Santo Domingo" seen sometimes on Dominican Republic coffee bags, do not indicate the coffee variety, it's the commercial brand name for coffee exported from the country.

About	The Dominican Republic (DR)
Area	18,791 sq mi (48,670 km²)
Population	10M
Taste	Barahona and Juncalito have a perfect balance between medium acidity and unique sweetness, which is reminiscent of the Jamaican Blue Mountain, with heavy body and good aroma. Other brands have medium body, light acidity and a slight chocolate taste with a shade of nuts and a nice aftertaste that remains in the mouth for a long time
Preferred roast	City to Full-city for Barahona and Juncalito brands and Full-city for the others
Washed or Unwashed	Washed
Classification	By region

Photo: Ben Garland, Coffee drying, Maquipucuna Reserve, Ecuador

ECUADOR

Located in the northern part of South America on the Pacific Ocean coast, Ecuador is rated among the top 20 coffee producing countries in the world. About 65% of Ecuadorian coffee is Arabica and the rest is Robusta. Almost half of the Arabica coffee comes from the western part of the country near the coast of Manabí, a very low altitude area, less than 2,300 ft (700 m), that produces poor quality coffee. More Arabica comes from El Oro and Loja in the south of the country. Most of the Robusta comes from Orellana, Los Rios and Sucumbios counties northeast to the capital of Quito.

The quality of Ecuadorian Arabica and Robusta coffee is considered poor to medium and is used mainly in industrial coffee.

The cultivation methods in Ecuador are not unified, each region using a different method, usually limited to primitive cultivation. It's possible to find both washed and unwashed coffee from Ecuador.

Most of the coffee is exported to the U.S. and to Europe to be incorporated into coffee blends, and the rest is marketed around the world as organic coffee.

Photo: Lena Struwe, coffee seedlings again, Maquipucuna Preserve, Ecuador

Ecuadorian coffee has high-medium acidity and medium body. Because of the unexceptional quality, its price is low. Gourmet Arabica coffee from Ecuador is a good supplement for espresso.

About	Ecuador
Area	109,483 sq mi (283,561 km^2)
Population	15M
Taste	Medium-bodied, with a medium to high acidity with a hint of fruit flavor
Preferred roast	Full-city
Washed or Unwashed	Both washed and unwashed
Classification	By defects, by screen size

EL SALVADOR

With a population of six million, the small Central American country of El Salvador produces more than 1.2 million bags per year and is rated around the 15th in the world. The government

Photo: Dan Iserman, Coffee Mill in El Salvador

doesn't invest enough in the coffee industry to improve the coffee quality and therefore quality is medium to low and intended for industrial use.

Coffee from El Salvador that grows on mountain slopes facing the ocean, under the same ideal climate conditions should be similar to Guatemalan coffee, its northern neighbor. But the ongoing civil war and elite government that employs natives under slavery-like conditions hindered the development of modern cultivation and sorting methods until 1992. In recent years there's been some improvement in the coffee quality, but there's still a long way to go.

Most of the El Salvadoran coffee is Arabica that comes from the Apaneca-Ilamatepec mountains in the southwest and from Tecapa-Chinameca in the southeast of the country. The small amount of good

Photo: Erik Törner, San Jorge estate, organic plantation, El Salvador

quality coffee produced in El Salvador is generally rated as Strictly Hard Bean (SHB) from trees that grow at altitudes higher than 3,900 ft (1,200 m). Brand names such as Tizapa and Pipil appear under the general name, "El Salvador High Grown."

Mixing El Salvador coffee with Indonesian or Papua New Guinea coffee provides good, rich espresso blends.

About	El Salvador
Area	8,125 sq mi (21,041 km²)
Population	6M
Taste	The quality coffee is quite similar to the Mexican coffee, without any significant features, with medium acidity, body and aroma. The taste is very soft with a nice sensation in the mouth that disappears quickly
Preferred roast	Problematic. On one hand a deep roasting into the second crack is recommended, but any slight deviation causes rapid coffee burning, and loss of the entire aroma. It takes a few tests to reach the accurate time needed to obtain quality coffee
Washed or Unwashed	Mostly washed
Classification	By altitude, defects and region/estate

ETHIOPIA

A landlocked country in East Africa, Ethiopia is known as the "origin" of the Arabica tree. (Uganda is considered the origin of Robusta). Coffee cultivation there began somewhere in the Caffa district, about 125 miles (200 km) southwest of its capital Addis-Ababa. Natives claim the source of the term "coffee" came from the district's name. Ethiopia is a third world country, not yet industrial, and its demographic structure is based on tribes spread all over the country.

The income of about 10% of the population depends on coffee farming. Most fruit is picked from wild uncultivated coffee trees, and the tribal distribution makes it difficult to control the coffee quality or its amount. However, despite the political difficulties and poverty in the country, Ethiopia succeeds in maintaining its place as one of the largest coffee growers in the world, producing more than 6 million bags of good Arabica coffee per year, half of which is exported. The coffee yield increases every year.

Ethiopian coffee grows mainly in the regions of Harrar in the east, Yirgacheffe, Sidamo and Bebeka in the south and Djimma (pronounced "Jimma"), Teppi, Limu and Lekempti in the west.

Photo: Oroma coffee producer: bunaoromiacoffee.co.uk

The most well-known gourmet coffee from Ethiopia, washed Yirgacheffe, is considered one of the best in the world and grows at an altitude of 5,580-6,250 ft (1,700-1,900 m).

The best unwashed coffee from Harrar, known as organic coffee, grows at an altitude of 5,250-6,560 ft (1,600-2,000 m) and is recognized by its yellow, almost golden, large sized beans. Sidamo is another variety also in high demand.

Adding Ethiopian coffee to South American coffee increases the overall acidity creating a sharper blend.

About	Ethiopia
Area	426,372 sq mi (1,104,300 km²)
Population	94M
Taste	Good acidity with fruit flavor. The Harrar coffee has sharp acidity, good body and wine-like taste whereas Sidamo has good acidity, Djimma has medium acidity and both have good body with good aftertaste
Preferred roast	Should be roasted carefully to City because it's easily burnt creating a bad taste
Washed or Unwashed	Both washed and unwashed
Classification	By defects, and region

GUATEMALA

Although one of the smallest countries in Central America, Guatemala is one of the top ten coffee exporters in the world. The climate in Antigua Heights, southwest of its capital Guatemala City at an altitude of 5,200 ft (1,600 m) is ideal for coffee cultivation. The Antigua brand, grown in this area, is considered one of the best in the world.

Most of the Guatemalan coffee is Arabica although a small amount of pretty good washed Robusta is grown on the Pacific Coast.

In additional to Antigua, other regions are famous for their coffee, Coban, Huehuetenango, Fraijanes, Atitlan and San Marcos. One of the advantages of Guatemalan coffee is the diverse possibilities of roasting levels. The flavor obtained at each roasting level is so different that Guatemalan coffee is in favor among roasting fans.

About	Guatemala
Area	42,042 sq mi (108,889 km^2)
Population	14M
Taste	The washed process results in a medium body, good acidity and a slight bitter chocolate flavor with a smoky background shadow. Leaves a good flavored aftertaste in the mouth
Preferred roast	City to Full-city and even somewhat longer to emphasize its chocolate flavor
Washed or Unwashed	Washed
Classification	By altitude, defects and region

HAWAII

The climate conditions of North America don't enable coffee cultivation. However, the conditions of Puerto Rico and the Hawaiian Islands allow the U.S. to become a coffee producer, even though the

Kona coffee plantation

Hawaiian state (an archipelago with eight main islands) is located 2,390 miles (3,850 km) from the west Pacific Ocean coast. The island of Kona produces one of the most famous and expensive coffees in the world. Due to a very large demand, it's difficult to obtain pure Kona coffee and there are therefore many frauds and forgeries. Many retailers confuse the consumers by preparing blends called Kona, but the original Kona quantity in these blends is often minimal. In recent years there have been other good coffee brands from Hawaii such as Molokai and Maui that are less expensive than Kona, but have quite a similar taste.

The coffee on the Big Island (Hawaii) is grown on the slopes of Mauna Loa, Mauna Kea and hualalai, all volcanic mountains. The extensive cloudy weather and reduced solar radiation provide greenhouse-like conditions and together with good precipitation result in excellent quality coffee.

Kona plantation size grader

The washed processing method is used in Hawaii and the coffee beans obtained are clean and somewhat flat.

Hawaiian coffee can be used as a single origin.

About	Hawaii
Area	10,930 sq mi (28,311 km²)
Population	1.4M
Taste	Delicate, with medium body and good acidity, its excellent aftertaste remains in the mouth long after drinking the coffee
Preferred roast	Between City to Full-city
Washed or Unwashed	Washed
Classification	By defects

HONDURAS

With a population of more than 8 million, Honduras is a relatively small country in Central America, but ranked around eighth in worldwide coffee production. Their coffee production has increased more than tenfold since 1970 and most of it is exported. It's one of the poorest countries in Central America and exporting coffee and bananas has improved its economy.

Most of the Honduran coffee comes from the northwest region of Santa Barbara, bordering Guatemala, from the southwestern region of El Paraiso, bordering Nicaragua and from the Comayagua region west of the Honduras capital, Tegucigalpa.

The highest quality and best crop is obtained from coffee plantations at the highest growing regions. The Honduran government does its best to improve both the yield and coffee quality.

Photo: Courtesy Counter Culture Coffee, patio drying at the Finca el Puente wet mill

About	Honduras
Area	43,278 sq mi (112,090 km²)
Population	8.3M
Taste	Considered medium-good without any particular features, with medium aroma and acidity and weak body
Preferred roast	City
Washed or Unwashed	Mostly washed, sometimes unwashed
Classification	By altitude and defects

INDIA

This big Asian country with more than 5 million bags per year (67% Robusta), is one of the largest coffee exporters in the world. Most of the coffee grown in India is of low quality, sold mainly to the industrial market. However, in recent years, it has also grown quality Arabica coffee.

Indian coffee is grown in the southwest part of the country in three states, mainly in Karnataka, with more than half of the Indian coffee, and in Kerala and Tamil Nadu. When first tasted, Indian coffee can be mistaken for Indonesian coffee. To notice the difference it has to be compared to Java coffee. Despite the similarity in body, Indian coffee has a piquant zest that contributes a special shade to its taste. The best quality Indian coffee is the strong and wild Monsoon. This coffee is processed in a special way that gives it a unique taste. After removing the skin from the unwashed Arabica coffee fruit,

Photo: Eduardo Iturrate. A local coffee shop

the green beans are placed in the open air on the ground in a layer of about 6-8" (15-20 cm). Workers continuously turn the beans to increase evaporation. After several days (three to seven, depending on the weather), the coffee beans are packed in sacks organized in rows to enable the Monsoon wind to blow between them.

Every few days the sacks are shaken and reorganized to get a uniform result. After six to eight weeks the beans' color changes to golden-yellow and they're fully "Monsooned."

Indian Robusta coffee is very good for making Turkish coffee. Adding Indian Arabica coffee to South American coffee adds body and decreases its acidity, creating a pungent blend.

Michael Reiner

Indian Truck Driver - Coorge, Karnataka, India

About	India
Area	1,269,214 sq mi (3,287,263 km^2)
Population	~1,200M
Taste	Monsoon coffee has a strong pungent taste
Preferred roast	Full-city to Vienna or even darker
Washed or Unwashed	Both washed and unwashed
Classification	By label, screen size and defects

INDONESIA

A population of 245 million Indonesians live on 6,000 islands of the largest archipelago in the world (17,000 islands). Coffee is grown on 12 of them. Indonesia in south Asia competes with Colombia as the third largest coffee supplier in the world, with more than 6

Photo: MTC Group, Flores Papawui UPH Sulawesi

million bags exported each year, about 5% of the world yield. 85-90% of Indonesian production is Robusta, and it is one of the largest producers of Robusta. The unique Indonesian Arabica has a high worldwide demand.

Some farmers store their coffee in storage houses for two or three years to age. The storage reduces acidity, increases body and creates a unique taste. The meaning of "body" in coffee is understood only after tasting aged coffee for the first time. The coffee is viscid and recalls the taste of brown olive oil, the smell is strong and the aroma spreads slowly in the mouth and lingers long after drinking.

Aged Indonesian coffee is more expensive than its fresh counterpart. Indonesian coffee can be used as a single origin to produce a very strong and pungent beverage, but is frequently used to reduce acidity and increase body in coffee blends.

Currently, the main sources of Indonesian coffee are from four Indonesian islands: Java, Sumatra, Sulawesi and Bali. There are differences in coffee features between these islands. Following are detailed descriptions of these four.

Photo: Troy Davis, coffee flower. www.animalcoffee.com

Indonesia basic information:

About	Indonesia
Area	735,355 sq mi (1,904,569 km²)
Population	245M
Taste	Typical great Indonesia Taste Full body, low acidity and a slight shade of earth and trees fragrance that remains in the mouth long after drinking
Classification	By defects, size and regions

JAVA - Indonesia

The island of Java is located east of Sumatra. With a population of more than 132 million, Java is the most populated island in the world. In the 17th century Dutch immigrants began to grow coffee trees on Java, making it the largest coffee producer in the world for the next 100 years. But tree diseases caused a drastic decrease in the yield. To overcome the problem, they planted Robusta, the more resistant trees. In recent years, some growers have started to grow Arabica. Many recognize "Java" as a synonym for coffee.

Growers use the washed method that reduces the body and adds a slight acidity. It doesn't have the common features of Indonesian coffee (especially in coffee from Sumatra and Sulawesi, which contains a shade of grass or forest moss, probably because other islands use the dry method). It's customary in Java to age part of the coffee harvest for one or two years.

Most of the Arabica is grown on the volcanic Ijen Plateau, in the east of Java. A small amount of quality Arabica, Java Preanger, is grown in the west of the island. Good Java Robusta coffee brands are Dampit and Estate, grown in the east.

Java coffee is sponsored by the government ("Government Estate") and marketed as Java with several sub-brandings such as Blawan, Jampit, Kayumas and also the well-known coffee "Kopi Luwak" (see Kopi Luwak chapter, page 144).

About	Java
Taste	Medium acidity with good aroma and medium body with a shade of smoke and a pinch of nut flavor
Preferred roast	To obtain good coffee dark roasted to Full-city or even Viennese. For those who like experimenting, it's recommended to try a less dark roast
Washed or Unwashed	Washed

SULAWESI - Indonesia

The large Indonesian island of Sulawesi (former Celebes), west of Java, produces Robusta and good Arabica.

In the center of the south peninsula of Sulawesi is the Tana Toraja Highland, at an altitude

Photo: MTC Group, Bone Bone, Enrekang Sulawesi

of 3,300-5,250 ft (1000-1600 m), where the best Indonesian Arabica coffee, Kalosi and Toraja is grown. A medium quality Robusta coffee is grown in the southern part of the peninsula.

About	Sulawesi
Taste	Toraja and Kalosi have medium body, good aroma, and a slight bitterness. Toraja has medium acidity, Kalosi has medium-low acidity
Preferred roast	Full-city
Washed or Unwashed	Washed

Photo: MTC Group, Local pulping

SUMATRA - Indonesia

Most of the Sumatran coffee is of medium quality. The good Robusta is Lampung from the north of the country. A small amount of good Arabica is grown in north Sumatra in three main regions: Mandheling, (considered one of the best in the world,) Lintong and Gayo. On December 24, 2004, a catastrophic tsunami hit the shores of Sumatra, damaging coffee production.

Photo: MTC Group, Sukamaju Subak Abian, cooperative processing station

About	Sumatra
Taste	Tasting Sumatran coffee, especially Mandheling, for the first time without expecting its strange taste may come as an unpleasant surprise. Not everyone can get used to its taste. It has a strong body, very low acidity and a touch of bitterness that stings the tongue. The aftertaste of grass sweetness lingers for a long time
Preferred roast	Its yellow color darkens uniformly and slowly during roasting. It's recommended to remove the beans from the heat source when most of the beans are at the same color
Washed or Unwashed	Both washed and unwashed

Photo: MTC Group, Coffee grinder, Bali Kintamani

BALI - Indonesia

Located southeast of Java, Bali is a relatively small island in comparison to the larger Indonesian islands such as Sumatra or Java. Nevertheless, it's populated by almost 4 million people – many of them coffee farmers. Most of the coffee is grown on volcanic soil. Good quality Arabica is grown in Kintamani Highland in the north and Robusta in Bali-Pupuan in the center. The coffee is sold in advance mainly to Japan, and the rest, which is in very high demand, is sold around the world for a high price.

The coffee, processed by the washed method, is clean and beautiful. Shinzan, one of the Kintamani brand names, is the best species in the country.

About	Bali
Taste	Kintamani is quite similar to other Indonesian coffee species with medium to high acidity and significant body. Very clean and smooth. Robusta Papuan has very high body with low acidity and little bit of sweetness
Preferred roast	City
Washed or Unwashed	Washed

IVORY COAST (CÔTE D'IVOIRE)

The Ivory Coast is a poor country on the western shore of Africa. It produces only Robusta coffee. Its main coffee regions are Aboisso, Divo and Abengourou. Since 1999 there's been a dramatic decrease in coffee production – from 5 million bags in 1999 to 1.5 million bags in 2012. This lower quantity is still enough to place it among the largest

Photo: Tom Neuhaus, Freshly roasted ground Robusta

15 coffee producers in the world, but its revenue is low because of the medium quality.

About	Ivory Coast
Area	124,503 sq mi (322,463 km²)
Population	22M
Taste	Full aroma, medium to low acidity and body
Preferred roast	Viennese and French
Washed or Unwashed	Unwashed
Classification	By screen size and by defects

JAMAICA

The high quality coffee of the small Caribbean island of Jamaica is world known. Many coffee fans are ready to pay five to tenfold for JBM (Jamaica Blue Mountain) coffee because of its exceptional taste. This coffee is considered by many to be the best coffee in the world. Some are willing to pay any price for it, especially in Japan that purchases most of it. Until about 20 years ago JBM coffee was considered unique, but in recent years it lost some of its uniqueness, maybe because of a wide variety of excellent specialty coffee. However, the demand is still higher than the supply and its price is as high as ever.

Historians say that in 1728 Nicholas Lewis, the governor of Jamaica, planted the first Arabica trees that became one of Jamaica's most profitable businesses. JBM, the turquoise color coffee, grows in the Blue Mountain region in the east of the country and is marketed worldwide. Most of JBM green coffee beans are packed and shipped in wooden barrels, in contrast to other countries that sell green coffee in sacks.

There are other Jamaican coffee brands grown in other areas, but only JBM is considered the best.

Located in eastern Jamaica, a constant mist covers the mountain range that rises to a height of 2,250 meters, its lush greenery creating the bluish shade that gives the range its name.

One of the questions asked by many coffee fans is what makes JMB coffee so good? It's assumed that the reduced sunlight caused by the mist, combined with low soil nutrients such as phosphorus and nitrogen forces the coffee tree to muster an increased effort to grow. The process is similar to wine, where the best grapes are grown in the harshest conditions. JBM coffee is very good as a single origin, but many coffee shops use JBM in blends to improve the taste.

About	Jamaica
Area	4,243 sq mi (10,991 km^2)
Population	3M
Taste	Strong fragrance, full body and excellent aroma. It has a slight sweetness and delicate acidity, and an aftertaste that lingers in the mouth for a long time
Preferred roast	It's important not to roast Jamaican coffee for too long. Recommended roasting is City. Remove from the heat source after the first crack. Continuing to the second crack may cause loss of the nice sweetness. Wait two days before using the roasted beans
Washed or Unwashed	Washed
Classification	By screen size, sometimes with an Estate name

KENYA

Kenya is located on the equator in eastern Africa. There, on the mountain slopes and in the high hilly region, native tribes grow one of the best Arabica varieties in the world. Coffee lovers appreciate the positive traits of Kenyan coffee. Kenyan

Photo: MTC Group, roasting before cupping

authorities are very strict regarding coffee quality, which guarantees the quality of exported coffee. The majority of the coffee is grown by small farmers, many of them organized as cooperatives, producing 20-300 bags per season. The harvested beans are gathered in processing centers. The packaged beans are then transported to the government center in the capital, Nairobi. Before releasing the coffee for sale, each batch of bags is graded for quality and bean size by authorized cuppers.

Then the real show begins. Once a week (since 1935) the coffee is sold in a public auction. Due to a tough competition between buyers, the coffee quality has improved.

Kenya's main growing regions are around Mount Kenya, north of Nairobi

Photo: MTC group, small round

and around the Kerio Valley National Park in the west. Estate Kenya, the Kenyan quality coffee, is very expensive and in high demand around the world.

Kenya produces about 800,000 bags per year and is ranked around 20th in the world. Weather changes and diseases have had a severe effect on quality coffee production in Kenya. The reduction in coffee production harmed many families that make their living from coffee farming.

A balanced good complex blend is obtained by mixing Kenyan coffee with Indonesian Mandheling coffee.

Photo: MTC Group, Thika coffee Mills drying tables

Photo: MTC Group, SDV Transami warehousing facility

About	Kenya
Area	224,080 sq mi (580,367 km^2)
Population	43M
Taste	Very rich, with high acidity, strong fragrance, medium body and a shade of fruity aftertaste that remains in the mouth long after drinking
Preferred roast	Full-city or the beginning of the second crack
Washed or Unwashed	Washed
Classification	Quality and size

MADAGASCAR

This gigantic island in the Indian Ocean, adjacent to the east shore of Southern Africa, is the fourth-largest island in the world. According to researchers, Madagascar was part of the African continent in the past. Today, it's considered a third world country.

Photo: Sarada Krishnan, coffee grafting, FOFIFA genebank nursery in Kianjavato, Madagascar

The poor living conditions, malnutrition and diseases of its 23 million people are among the worst in the world. The majority of the people make their living from agriculture and coffee is one of the most important crops in the country. Almost all the coffee grows wild and is picked by smallholders, very small family-owned farms. Until 1960, when it became independent, Madagascar was part of the French Colonial Empire.

Coffee grows all over the island, mainly in the center highlands. The rainy weather throughout the year enables the coffee to grow wild in remote and inaccessible places. Most of the coffee crop (more than 95%) is Robusta. Only 30% of the coffee is exported because of its low quality. A small amount of good Arabica is exported as organic coffee.

About	Madagascar
Area	22.666 sq mi (58,7041 km²)
Population	23M
Taste	Arabica has high acidity, strong aroma and medium body. Robusta has medium acidity and body with a slight bitterness and low aroma
Preferred roast	Arabica should be roasted to Full-city and Robusta to Viennese
Washed or Unwashed	Unwashed
Classification	By screen size and number of defects

MEXICO

With a production of more than 4 million coffee bags per year, Mexico is among the 10 largest exporters in the world. However, it suffers from one of the common problems in the coffee market known as "unmarked." Namely, the coffee is graded as inferior quality. Before buying Mexican coffee one should check carefully whether it's graded

Coffee shop at San Cristobal de las Casas, Mexico

or cheap, unmarked coffee. On the other hand, because of the primitive cultivation, some of the Mexican coffee is organic. Most of the Mexican coffee is purchased by the U.S. Over 90% of the Mexican coffee growers are small farms of about 5-12 acres (20-50 dunam). The workers live under harsh conditions in floorless huts with poor sanitation.

The main coffee regions in Mexico are in the southern part of the country. The well-known Veracruz and Coatepec coffee are grown in the mountains near the Gulf bay and other good quality coffee is grown in Chiapas and Oaxaca regions.

About	Mexico
Area	758,446 sq mi (1,964,375 km²)
Population	115M
Taste	Mostly medium body, medium acidity and a nutty shade. Coffee from Chiapas and Oaxaca has medium body and acidity with fruity flavor and chocolate hints. The coffee from Coatepec and Veracruz regions has a different taste from other Central American crops and has higher acidity with a flowery flavor
Preferred roast	Full-city, until the beginning of the second crack
Washed or Unwashed	Mostly washed
Classification	By altitude and defects

NICARAGUA

The government of the Central American country of Nicaragua began to rehabilitate the coffee market and recover its national economy only after the end of the cruel civil war in 1990.

Nava writz, Coffee house, Nicaragua

Most of Nicaragua coffee (Arabica) is grown in small farms less than 7 acres (30 dunam).

More than 85% of the Nicaraguan coffee grows in three regions in the north: Jinotega, Matagalpa and Nueva Segovia, at an altitude from 2,500-5,500 ft (750-1700 m).

About	Nicaragua
Area	50,336 sq mi (130,370 km²)
Population	6M
Taste	Good acidity and medium body with a nutty flavor, sometimes combined with a hint of chocolate
Preferred roast	City to Full-city
Washed or Unwashed	Washed
Classification	By region altitude and defects

PANAMA

The small country in Central America with a population of less than 4 million is known in the world for its canal connecting the Atlantic and the Pacific oceans and for its coffee production. Panama produces a small amount of coffee per year, around 100,000 bags (60 kg), half of it for export.

In July 2013 two buyers (from Japan and Taiwan,) won the "Best of Panama" online auction and paid $350.25 per pound for Panama "Esmeralda Special" coffee from the Hacienda la Esmeralda farm in the Panama province of Chiriqui.

The winning grade motivated coffee farmers to produce even better coffee. The quality and taste of Arabica from Panama competes with big names such as Hawaiian Kona, Costa Rican coffee and even with Jamaican Blue Mountain, but its price is more reasonable.

Photo: Rich Helms, coffeetroupe.com, worker carry a 75lb bag

Most of the coffee in the country is grown in the western mountainous Chiriquí Province, at an altitude of 4,000 ft (1200 m). The environmental conditions are ideal for growing perfect coffee. One of the best brand names from this region is Boquete. Panama classifies their best coffee as SHB (Strictly Hard Bean) accompanied by the farm names or province, for example La Torcaza, Carmen, Hartmann Estate, Maunier.

About	Panama
Area	29,120 sq mi (75,420 km²)
Population	3.6M
Taste	Balanced between good acidity and full body, supplemented with fruity sweetness
Preferred roast	City roasting, without continuing any further to avoid spoilage of the unique bean taste
Washed or Unwashed	Washed
Classification	By density (altitude) and region/estate

PAPUA NEW GUINEA

The huge New Guinea Island, located about 185 miles (300 km) north of Australia, is divided between Indonesia in the north (known as Irian Jaya) and PNG (Papua New Guinea) in the south.

Coffee was introduced to the country by local inhabitants at the beginning of the twentieth century from Jamaica and the plants developed well. Local farmers

Photo: MTC Group, Collecting coffee beans, PNG

cultivate coffee by simple, primitive methods and many coffee lovers seek this coffee, considering it to be real organic coffee.

Photo: MTC Group, Sorting cherry, PNG

More than 85% PNG coffee is high-grown Arabica along the highlands from east to west. Some PNG varieties are so good they compete with the Jamaica Blue Mountain. PNG coffee brand names are either derived from the growth district such as Arona, Wahgi, Kimel or Sigri or simply PNG organic or PNG Peaberry.

About	Papua New Guinea
Area	178,702 sq mi (462,840 km²)
Population	6.5M
Taste	High quality Arabica has a strong body and aroma, medium acidity and a sensation of fruit sweetness, without the taste of soil that accompanies other Indonesian species
Preferred roast	Between City to Full-city shortly after the first crack
Washed or Unwashed	Washed
Classification	By defects

PERU

The country of Peru in the west of South America is surrounded by the Pacific Ocean on the west side and the Andes Mountains on the east. Coffee is grown all over the country in more than 12 districts including Cajamarca, Amazonas,

Photo: Santa Teresa plantation, Peru

San Martín provinces in the north, Chanchamayo in the center and Cusco, Ayacucho and Puno provinces in the south. More than 100,000 small farmers each cultivate around 2 acres (8 dunam) growing their coffee on the high slopes of the Andes, under ideal climate conditions.

Peru is one of the largest producers of organic coffee in South America. Because of its relatively low price, organic coffee lovers are attracted to it, more because it is label "organic" rather than because of it's quality. Peru increases its coffee production constantly and is now four-times higher than in 1993.

It's commonly branded as "Organic coffee from Peru," indicating the name of the district it comes from. The best known organic coffee, also called Fruiter, is from the district of Cajamarca, east of the capital Lima.

About	Peru
Area	496,222 sq mi (1,285,216 km²)
Population	30M
Taste	The best quality coffee from Peru has a high aroma, medium acidity, medium body and contains fruity shades
Preferred roast	Darker roasting (Viennese) provides strong acceptable coffee
Washed or Unwashed	Washed
Classification	By size and defects

RWANDA

The very small landlocked country in East Africa, Rwanda, is surrounded by Tanzania, Burundi, Uganda and the Democratic Republic of the Congo. About 800,000 Tutsis were killed in the 1994 civil war shocking the world in an act that can be described as "genocide." As a result of this war the coffee production decreased by about 15-fold in 1995.

Coffee production in Rwanda began to improve just a few years later when the government opened the market to free trade. It recently became well-known and in high demand. The mountainous country of Rwanda is called "Land of a Thousand Hills." These mountains, higher than 5,000 ft (1,500 m), provide ideal conditions for coffee cultivation. About 500,000 families make their living from coffee. Rwanda exports both quality and inferior coffee. Because of the unique grading method that includes impairments, tasting and general impression, coffee from Rwanda is considered one of the best in Africa. Due to its traits that are similar to African coffee, the demand for Rwandan coffee is high. Those who are fond of African coffee will enjoy it.

Rwandan coffee production is Arabica. The best Rwandan coffee is Maraba.

About	Rwanda
Area	10,169 sq mi (26,338 km²)
Population	12M
Taste	Strong body, smoothness and clear acidity with a strong floral fragrance and tone. Maraba coffee contains a slight sweetness and its aftertaste lingers in the mouth long after drinking
Preferred roast	City
Washed or Unwashed	Washed and semi-washed
Classification	By cupping and brand name

TANZANIA

Tanzania is located on the eastern shore of Africa. Among the country's more than 44 million poor people, about half of them make their living from agriculture, and coffee is one of the most significant products.

Photo: Ron Jones, Coffee plantation, Gibb's farm, Tanzania

Good Tanzanian coffee is grown in three regions: around Mt. Kilimanjaro, Bukoba, Mt. Menu and Mbeya. More than 85% of the Tanzanian coffee is supplied by small family farms, each one up to three acres (4-12 dunam). About 50-60% of the coffee is Arabica, processed by the washed method and the rest is Robusta, processed by the unwashed method. The special Tanzanian species is Peaberry (one bean in each cherry).

The most famous Tanzanian Arabica coffee is Kilimanjaro that grows at a very high altitude on the slopes of the highest mountain in Africa.

About	Tanzania
Area	365,753 sq mi (947,300 km²)
Population	44M
Taste	Typical African, with medium body, strong acidity and a winey shade
Preferred roast	The recommended roasting is Full-city or more, toward the Viennese
Washed or Unwashed	Washed and unwashed
Classification	By defects and screen size

UGANDA

Winston Churchill labeled Uganda "The African Pearl." The water abundance in the rivers, waterfalls and lakes, over 500 conserved forests populated by rare and unique animals, combined with idyllic climate, deem it one of

Photo: Sarah McCans, Women Sorting Coffee Beans

the most beautiful countries in the world. The central African landlocked country borders Rwanda, the Democratic Republic of the Congo, Sudan, Kenya and Tanzania. In 1962 Uganda obtained its independence, but in 1971, after a military coup, the dictator Idi Amin declared himself president of Uganda. Its economy collapsed under his administration, and the coffee production decreased until 1979 when Yoweri Museveni took the lead. Under his leadership the country regained its stability and the economy continues to improve today.

Photo Rachel Strohm, House Coffee, Kampala, Uganda

Uganda is considered the origin of Robusta (Ethiopia is considered the origin of Arabica), and has a long tradition of coffee production. Unique species of wild Robusta trees can still be found in the rainforests.

Old stories tell of Ugandan natives chewing coffee beans before combat to feel stronger, braver and undefeatable. Uganda is one of the 10 largest coffee producers in the world, with around

4 million bags per year, and is ranked first in organic coffee production in Africa. About 80% of the coffee produced in Uganda is Robusta and only 20% is Arabica. With more than 15% of the population connected in one way or another to coffee production, it's naturally one of the main income sources of foreign currency to the country. Most of their production is favored and marketed in Europe.

The traditionally dry-processed Robusta coffee is known for its good quality, whereas the quality of Arabica coffee is medium. In recent years the Ugandan government successfully attempted to improve the quality of the Arabica to obtain higher revenue.

Coffee in Uganda is grown all over the country. Main coffee regions are around Lake Victoria in the south, near Rwenzori Mountains in the west, near the border of the Democratic Republic of the Congo and around Mount Elgon in the east on the border of Kenya, where the known Bugisu coffee variety originates. Other known Arabica varieties are Wugar and Drugar.

About	Uganda
Area	93,065 sq mi (241,038 km^2)
Population	36M
Taste	Ugandan Robusta features are vigorous. It has full body, bubbling acidity and unique sweetness. Bugishu variety has strong acidic, with medium body, full aroma and leaves a slight aftertaste of fruit fragrance
Preferred roast	Full-city roasting is recommended for Robusta, and City roasting is recommended for Arabica varieties
Washed or Unwashed	Arabic washed, Robusta unwashed
Classification	By screen size, defects and region

VENEZUELA

Coffee production in Venezuela, the northern South American country, was neglected up until about 40 years ago because of the fast and high profit from petroleum. In recent years the government decision to invest money in coffee farming brought about a positive change in the coffee quality.

Photo: David B. Fankhauser, Professor, UC Clermont College,
http://biology.clc.uc.edu/fankhauser/

Most of the Venezuelan coffee is grown in Portuguesa and Lara states in the west central part of the country. Coffee is also grown in Cordillera de Mérida, in the northeastern part of the country and on the slopes of the Andes extension – Táchira and Mérida.

About	Venezuela
Area	352,143 sq mi (912,050 km²)
Population	28M
Taste	Venezuelan coffee is not similar to Colombian coffee. It has a lower acidity, a slight sweetness and a medium to high body
Preferred roast	The recommended roasting is a little more after the Full-city, toward Viennese roasting
Washed or Unwashed	Washed and unwashed
Classification	By defects and regions

VIETNAM

In Southeast Asia, with a population of more than 92 million, Vietnam demonstrates how a country government can turn coffee into a major income. The coffee production increased from 69,000 bags in 1984

Photo: copyright Rainforest Alliance

to 29 million in 2014 (an increase of 420-fold). Vietnam became a powerful coffee nation, second in the world after Brazil, supplying around 20% of the world consumption, most of it (96%) Robusta. However, because of its low quality and low price, Vietnamese coffee is exported mainly to the

instant coffee industry or used locally. The main coffee region, Tây Nguyên, known as the Central Highlands, close to the Cambodian border, includes five provinces (Đắk Lắk, Đắk Nông, Gia Lai, Kon Tum and Lâm Đồng). Coffee is also grown in the southeast Đông Nam Bộ and on the southern central coast (Nam Trung Bộ). In recent years there's been a small improvement in Vietnamese coffee quality and it continues to improve.

Vietnamese coffee is very good for Turkish coffee and also suitable for cold coffee and sweet beverages.

About	Vietnam
Area	127,880 sq mi (331,210 km²)
Population	92M
Taste	Vietnamese coffee has low acidity and strong aroma
Preferred roast	The recommended roasting is Viennese
Washed or Unwashed	Unwashed
Classification	By defects and screen size

YEMEN

Even though it's a relatively small coffee producer (around the thirtieth in the world), the unique taste of Yemen coffee requires special attention. It's not easy to describe the taste of Yemenite

Photo: Coffeeshrub, (www.coffeeshrub.com), Terraces for coffee, Harazi, Yemen

coffee, but it is undoubtedly, different! It's very special and complex, with strong body, and with high but different acidity than in other African or South American coffee. It contains a fruity and chocolate shade, but also some bitterness. Some people can't get used to this taste and others find it everything they're looking for.

Yemen, located geographically on the southern tip of the Arabian Peninsula, belongs to Asia, but its coffee taste and characteristics are closer to African and Arabian coffee. Contrary to some legends, coffee growers in Yemen believe that their country is the origin of Arabica, and not Ethiopia.

One of the most known Yemen coffee brands is Yemen Mocha (Also Mokha, Moca or Moka), which has nothing to do with the chocolatey mocha taste we know. It's named after a harbor in the Red Sea, from which coffee was exported to the world in the past. Today, most of the Yemenite coffee is shipped from Aden Harbor, but the brand is still called Mocha.

Yemenite coffee comes from the high mountains in the west of the country that stretch north to south. The coffee grows on terraces on the slopes at an altitude of 3,300-5,600 ft (1000-1700 m), under conditions of warm weather and enough rain that makes Yemen coffee so special and different in taste. Bani Matar, west of Yemen's capital Sana'a, is the main coffee growing region. Other coffee regions are, Jabal Bani Ismail, situated west to Bani Matar and the Haraz region in the southwest.

Because the coffee is grown under primitive conditions, including drying in the sun, it's considered organic coffee and is in high demand.
Yemenite coffee is relatively expensive. It can be used as a single origin, but because of its high acidity it's also suitable for blends with almost any kind of coffee.

About	Yemen
Area	203,848 sq mi (527,968 km²)
Population	25M
Taste	Strong body, high acidity and high aroma. It contains a fruity and chocolate shade, but also some bitterness
Preferred roast	Roasting of Yemenite coffee requires much skill and it's important to stop the roasting on time to avoid excess bitterness. It should be roasted to Full-city, just before the second crack, without relating to its color
Washed or Unwashed	Unwashed
Classification	By region

Photo: courtesy of Dave Rea daverea1978@yahoo.co.uk

COFFEE ESPRESSO MACHINE BUYER GUIDE

Now that you've made the decision to buy an espresso machine, you may be overwhelmed by the abundance of machines on the market. You definitely want to buy the best machine for the lowest price, but this presents a challenge. Buying an espresso machine is different than buying a refrigerator.

While a refrigerator can be found in any shop that sells appliances, and the salespeople have a certain amount of product knowledge, it takes a unique salesperson with specialized knowledge to sell an espresso machine.

The appliance can turn into a white elephant or an environmental nuisance if you purchase one that doesn't meet your needs.

If you're still uncertain which type of machine to choose, here's a simple tool to help you compare machine types, cost and performance.

SELECTION TABLE

In order to facilitate the buyer decision we will classify the espresso machines into 6 categories:

- **Lever** - Lever espresso machine.
- **Capsule** - Capsule / Pod Espresso Machine.
- **Basic** - Basic Semi-Automatic Espresso Machine, usually with Thermoblock or small boiler and a plastic housing.
- **Advanced** - Advanced Semi-automatic Espresso Machine (Stainless Steel Housing, Large boiler).
- **Professional** - Professional Espresso Machine (Heat exchanger, Stainless Steel Housing, Professional Brew Group (e.g. E61) and Commercial Style Portafilter.
- **Super Auto.** - Super Automatic Machine.

+ For Advanced Semi-automatic Espresso Machine and Professional Espresso Machine, purchasing an additional stand-alone coffee grinder is recommended.

*August 2015 prices

Question	Answer	Lever	Capsule	Basic	Advanced	Professional	Super Auto.
How much you are prepared to pay for the machine?	The cheapest, $300 max*		●	●			
	No more than $600*		●		●		●
	$1000 max*	●			●		●
	Price is not important	●				●	●
Where are you going to install the machine?	At home	●	●	●	●	●	●
	In the office		●				●
How many cups do you wish to prepare per day?	2-4 cups per day: 1 good espresso cup in the morning and 1-2 in the evening	●	●	●			
	6-8 cups per day				●		●
	Ten or more cups per day					●	●
Is simplicity important to you?	Yes, I'm usually in a rush and prefer to simply push a button		●				●
	No. I enjoy preparing quality coffee	●		●	●	●	
Is espresso quality important?	Very important	●+			●+	●+	
	Important, but not crucial		●	●			●
Is frothing quality critical for you?	Yes, I like good Cappuccino, like we get in a coffee shop				●	●	
	No, I drink mainly espresso, or I can use a standalone milk frother	●	●	●	●	●	●
Is coffee freshness important?	Very important	●+		●+	●+	●+	●
	Important, but not crucial		●	●			

QUESTIONNAIRE FOR CHOOSING ESPRESSO MACHINE

Ask yourself these questions before buying a new espresso machine. Also ask the salesperson for a demonstration before making the purchase. Not all features are appropriate for every espresso machine, and not every seller can supply answers to every question.

The last table is for super automatic machine.

General

Subject	Question / Remark	Note
Salesman	Selling espresso machines requires special expertise. Don't buy if the salesman isn't absolutely familiar with the product.	
Demo	It's recommended to buy in a store that offers demonstrations.	
Warranty	Is there a warranty? For how long? Usually the warranty is for one year.	Consider buying a machine with extended warranty, if possible.
Service	It's important to know the name of the service company, where it's located and the response time.	SLA = Service Level Agreement.
Accessories and gifts	What accessories come with the machine? Usually, you'll get extra filter baskets (for single & double shots), a tamper and a 0.25 oz (7g) measuring scoop. Some companies also add a pod filter basket adaptor or a milk frother such as Panarello or Cappuccinatore.	See Accessories, page 110

Specifications

Subject	Question / Remark	Note
Weight	Machine weight can provide a good clue as to whether the machine is professional.	Usually, a higher weight means more metal parts which are desirable.
Size	Ensure you have enough space for the machine. Check the directions for removable parts such as the water tank.	
Cup height	What is the highest cup size you intend to use? In some machines the tray can be removed to free up more space for the cup.	Some automatic machines are adjustable and enable the use of tall cups.
Power	Machine wattage	
Machine body material	Plastic, ABS, aluminum or stainless steel.	
Dripping tray	The material of the tray. How easily does it disassemble for cleaning?	

Heating system

Subject	Question / Remark	Note
Heating system	Thermoblock, single boiler, heat exchanger or two boilers.	See Heating methods in espresso machine, page 93
Boiler material	Aluminum, brass, copper or stainless steel.	
Boiler volume	Larger boiler volume provides better temperature stability and better steam for milk frothing, but, consumes more power and longer time for the first cup.	

The system - Mechanism

Subject	Question / Remark	Note
Pump	Does it contain a pump?	Check if it is not a steam machine. See page 83
Pump type	Vibration or rotary.	A rotary pump is available only in professional machines.
Three way solenoid valve	Check whether the machine is able to release pressure after making espresso.	See page 100
Pre-infusion	Does the machine inject a small amount of water upon beginning the extraction process?	

Portafilter

Subject	Question / Remark	Note
Material	Metal, wood, brass, aluminum, stainless steel.	
Diameter	Generally smaller diameter, less professional.	Standard diameter is 2.28" (58mm).
Weight	Portafilter weight reflects on the machine quality, the heavier the better.	
Number of filter handles	For single, double shot and a pod adapter.	With some machines you'll also get a blind filter.

Steam Wand

Subject	Question / Remark	Note
Steam wand length	Check the length.	It should fit the milk pitcher depth.
Steam wand position	Check whether it's suitable for the planned location.	Right or left.
Steam wand movement	Check the steam wand movement, whether it can move freely in all directions.	Does it have a ball joint?

Cold water tank

Subject	Question / Remark	Note
Water tank capacity	Most machines contain 34-68 oz (1-2 l).	
Additional water inlet	Is it necessary to remove the water tank for filling or does the machine have an additional water inlet?	
Scale filter	Does the water tank contain an integral scale filter? Is there an option to add one?	See Water Quality, page 103
Water level gauge	Does the machine have a water level gauge?	The machine should turn itself off automatically when the cold water tank empties.

Cup Warmer

Subject	Question / Remark	Note
Size of cup warmer	Is one available? And for how many cups?	
Passive or active	Passive means it's heated by the machine heat and active means it uses an independent heating source.	

Performance

Subject	Question / Remark	Note
Warm-up time	The time needed to stabilize the temperature and to prepare the first good shot.	
Steam building time	The time needed to build good steam for frothing.	For machines with one boiler.
Frothing time	The time needed to froth 7 oz (200 ml) of cold milk to 158oF (70oC).	20- 50 sec.
Steam potential	Can it froth milk for 2-4 cups without pausing?	

SuperAutomatic Machines

Subject	Question / Remark	Note
Digital display	Does the machine have a digital display?	
Failure control panel	Does it indicate specific problems or only a light indicating a problem?	Common failures: lack of water, disposal bin full, descaling, etc.
Pre-ground bypass doser	Does the machine include an additional inlet for ground coffee?	
Coffee beans hopper capacity	Small container means frequently adding beans.	Usually about 1/2 lb (250 gram).
Coffee grounds drawer capacity	How many cups you can make before it will be full.	Usually 8-12.
Cappuccino option	Is the machine able to prepare cappuccino automatically?	One touch.
Aroma selection	Can you control the amount of ground coffee in each cup?	

CUPPING FORM

Sample No.	Roast level	Aroma			Taste score 1-5 (1=Poor, 2=Fair, 3=Good, 4=Very Good, 5=Excellent)							General comments
		Ground coffee	Before breaking	After breaking	Flavor	Body	Acidity	Sweetness	Complexity	Aftertaste	Overall Taste	
1		L M H	L M H	L M H								
2		L M H	L M H	L M H								
3		L M H	L M H	L M H								
4		L M H	L M H	L M H								
5		L M H	L M H	L M H								
6		L M H	L M H	L M H								
7		L M H	L M H	L M H								
8		L M H	L M H	L M H								
9		L M H	L M H	L M H								
10		L M H	L M H	L M H								

L = low; M = medium; H = high

ROASTING STAGES

This table represents the roasting stages in a home roaster. (in industrial roasters the temperature profile is lower).
Each roaster performs differently dependent on the amount of beans, beans type, heating method and heating profile.
In spite of that, the roasting stages in all roasters are identical.

Stage	Color	Temp. °F	Temp. °C	Phenomenon	Weight loss	Volume increase	Acidity	Body	Aroma	Taste in the cup	Comments
First stage		365-380	185-195	Beans' color changes to random brown color with a grassy smell.	4%-6%	25%-40%			Irrelevant		Generally is not used for brewing.
Cinnamon		375-400	190-205	Beans' color is orange-brown and it smells like toasted bread.	5%-10%	30%-60%	H	L	M	High acidity.	The beans' sugars caramelize. A smell of toasted bread spreads in the air.
American		390-420	199-215	**The first crack** occurs, cracking noise can be heard.	8%-14%	50%-80%	H-M	M-L	H-M	Peak acidity. Aroma increases.	A good coffee smell.
City		410-435	210-224	The beans' color becomes unified brown, cracking noise can still be heard.	12%-18%	70%-90%	M	M	H	Acidity begins to decrease and the sweetness begins to emerge.	
Full-city		430-455	221-235	The beginning of **the second crack**, the beans look oily, the color is beautiful brown-black.	15%-18%	80%-100%	M	M-H	H	The aroma begins to decrease and the sweetness begins to turn into bitterness.	An unpleasant burnt coffee smell started.
Viennese		445-465	230-240	The second crack ends. The beans are filled with oil.	16%-20%	100%	M-L	H	M	The aroma is medium, almost without acidity, and the taste is bitter-sweet.	The oil burnt and smoke is starting to get out.
French/ Italian		455-475	235-246	There is almost no change in the beans' color but a smell of burnt oil is spread in the air.	18%-20%	100%	L	M	M	Very low aroma, no acidity, and the taste becomes bitter without sweetness.	Careful! A few seconds more and the beans will burn.
Burnt coffee		>480	>249		20%	100%			Irrelevant		You got coal.

Most of the color pictures from this book can be found at www.coffee-lovers-guide.com

212

COFFEE IN OTHER LANGUAGES

Enter a coffee shop in any country around the world and ask for coffee. The barista will probably understand your order, even if the word sounds different in his or her native language. Nevertheless, you'll get better results using the local language. Here are some common ways to order coffee in other languages.

Country	Language	Native language	Pronunciation
Albania and Kosovo	Albanian	**kafe**	**K**aafe
Armenian	Armenian	**սուրճ**	**S**oorj
Azerbaijan	Azerbaijani or Azeri	**qəhvə**	**Q**ahwa
Bangladesh and parts of India	Bengali or Bangla	**কফি**	Ka**phi**
Belarus	Belarusian	**кава**	**K**ava
Bosnia, Herzegovina and Montenegro	Bosnian	**Kahva**	**K**afe
Bulgaria	Bulgarian	**кафе**	kaa**FE**
Burundi	Kirundi / Rundi	**IKawa**	Eekavha
Cambodia	Khmer	**កាហ្វេ**	**G**ah**f**ay
China (Mandarin, Gan, Hakka, etc.)	Chinese	**咖啡**	**K**afeei
Croatia	Croatian	**kava**	**K**a**V**a
Czech Republic and Slovakia	Czech	**káva**	**K**aa**V**a
Denmark	Danish	**kaffe**	kaffe
Egypt	Egyptian	**kahwa**	**Q**ahwa
Estonia	Estonian	**kohv**	**K**o**ch**ee
Ethiopia	Amharic	**ቡና**	boona
Finland	Finnish	**kahvia**	**K**ahffi
France	French	**café**	**K**afe
Georgia	Georgian	**ყავა**	**Q**aava
Germany	German	**Kaffee**	**K**affee
Greece and Cyprus	Greek	**καφές**	**K**afes
Haiti	Haitian Creole	**kafe**	ka**FE**

Country	Language	Native language	Pronunciation
Hawaii (part of US)	Hawaiian	**Kope**	**K**ope
Hong Kong	Cantonese	咖啡	**G**a fei
Hungary	Hungarian	**kávé**	**K**ahave
Iceland	Icelandic	**kaffi**	**K**affi
India	Hindi	कॉफ़ी	**K**ofi
India	Kannada	ಕಾಫಿ	**KA**ffi
India	Gujarati	કૉફી	**KO**fi
India	Telugu	కాఫీ	**KA**ffi
Indonesia	Indonesian	**kopi**	**K**opii
Iran	Persian	قهوه	**K**achwee
Israel	Hebrew	קפה	**K**afe
Italy	Italian	**caffè**	**K**afeh
Japan	Japanese	コーヒー	**K**o-Hi
Kenya	Swahili	**kahawa**	**K**aha**W**a
Korea	Korean	커피	**K**eo**P**i
Laos	Lao	ກາເຟ	**K**ahafee
Madagascar	Malagasy	**café**	**K**afe
Malaysia	Malay	**kopi**	**K**opi
Most Arabic countries	Arabic	قهوة	**Q**ahwa
Netherlands	Dutch	**koffie**	**K**offie
Norway	Norwegian	**kaffe**	**K**afe
Papua New Guinea	Tok Pisin	**kopi**	**K**ofi
Philippines	Filipino (Tagalog)	**kape**	**K**a**PHE**
Poland	Polish	**kawa**	**K**ava
Portuguese countries	Portuguese	**café**	**K**afe
Republic of Latvia	Latvian	**kafija**	**K**afiy
Republic of Macedonia	Macedonian	**кафе**	**K**afe
Romania and Moldova	Romanian	**cafea**	**K**afea
Russia	Russian	**кафе**	**K**ofi
Rwandan	Kinyarwanda	**ikawa /ikâawâ**	EeKAHwah (Ikawa)
Serbia and Montenegro	Serbian	**кафе**	**K**a**F**a
Slovakia	Slovak	**káva**	**K**haava
South Africa	Afrikaans	**koffie**	**K**ofi

Country	Language	Native language	Pronunciation
Spain	Spanish	café	Kafe
Spain and Andora	Catalan	cafè	KaFe
Sri Lanka, India, Malaysia, Singapore and Mauritius	Tamil	காபி	Kaapi
Syria	Arabic	قهوة	HaaWa
Sweden	Swedish	kaffe	KaaFe
Thailand	Thai	กาแฟ	Kahafe
Turkey	Turkish	kahve	KahaVe
Ukraine	Ukrainian	Кави	Kavy
Vietnam	Vietnamese	cà phê	Ka_Fe
Yemen	Arabic	قهوة	Qahwa
Zimbabwe	Shona	kofi	Koffi

DATA ON WORLD COFFEE CONSUMPTION

AMOUNTS OF COFFEE PRODUCED IN THE WORLD

The following table presents the amount of coffee produced by the 15 largest exporting countries. The data refer to the reported amounts.

Many countries don't report on their coffee export or local coffee consumption. Therefore, much information regarding coffee yield, especially in East Asia, is missing. To date, the amount of coffee produced in China, mainly for local consumption, is unknown, but it's realistic to assume that it's not a negligible amount.

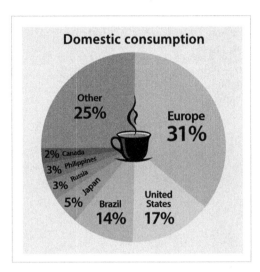

Domestic consumption

Other 25%
Europe 31%
2% Canada
3% Philippines
3% Russia
5% Japan
Brazil 14%
United States 17%

5 top coffee production countries in the world in recent years:

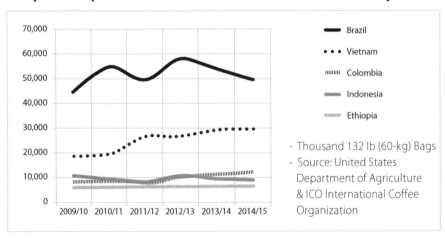

- Brazil
- Vietnam
- Colombia
- Indonesia
- Ethiopia

- Thousand 132 lb (60-kg) Bags
- Source: United States Department of Agriculture & ICO International Coffee Organization

Amount of coffee produced by the top 15 growing countries

Production	2010/11	2011/12	2012/13	2013/14	*2014/15	Arabica	Robusta	% Robusta	Exports
Brazil	54,500	49,200	57,600	54,500	51,200	34,200	17,000	33%	61%
Vietnam	19,415	26,000	26,500	29,833	29,350	1,100	28,250	96%	93%
Colombia	8,525	7,655	9,927	12,075	12,500	12,500	0	0%	89%
Indonesia	9,325	8,300	10,500	9,500	8,800	1,450	7,350	84%	65%
Ethiopia	6,125	6,320	6,325	6,345	6,350	6,350	0	0%	51%
India	5,035	5,230	5,303	5,075	5,100	1,400	3,700	73%	76%
Honduras	3,975	5,600	4,725	4,400	5,000	5,000	0	0%	96%
Uganda	3,212	3,075	3,600	3,850	4,000	800	3,200	80%	94%
Mexico	4,000	4,300	4,650	3,800	3,900	3,700	200	5%	43%
Guatemala	3,960	4,410	4,010	3,415	3,615	3,600	15	0%	83%
Peru	4,100	5,200	4,300	4,250	3,400	3,400	0	0%	95%
Nicaragua	1,740	2,100	1,925	1,850	1,850	1,850	0	0%	97%
Cote d'Ivoire	1,600	1,600	1,750	1,575	1,600	0	1,600	100%	88%
Malaysia	1,100	1,450	1,400	1,500	1,600	0	1,600	100%	50%
Costa Rica	1,575	1,775	1,675	1,425	1,525	1,525	0	0%	75%
Other	12,230	11,682	10,626	9,119	10,011	5,826	4,185		
Total	**140,417**	**143,897**	**154,816**	**152,512**	**149,801**				

- Thousand of 132 lb (60-kg) Bags
- Source: United States Department of Agriculture & ICO International Coffee Organization
* From Dec-2014

ADDITIONAL TASTE COMPONENTS

There are four known basic tastes in the world: sweet, bitter, sour and salty. Other taste terms used in the coffee world are: acidity, body, aroma, flavor and aftertaste (described in detail in the "Coffee Taste" chapter). There are also hundreds of professional tastes and sub-tastes terms that describe the large variety of coffee tastes.

Following are a concise list of commonly used taste terms mainly among coffee cuppers:

Term	Description
Acerbic	A flawed taste that feels bitter-sour on the tongue, produced by internal burn of coffee beans during slow cooling.
Ashy	Cigarette-like taste that remains in the mouth long after drinking coffee.
Astringent	A stinging sub-taste (also called pinching) when drinking coffee. Leaves a feeling of contraction on the tongue, especially when drinking Asian Robusta coffee.
Baked	A bland flat taste of coffee roasted for a long time at low temperature.
Balanced	A term used to describe a round coffee taste.
Bland	"Tasteless" coffee, either without traits or with very weak traits. It may be Arabica that has not been grown under optimal conditions or lightly roasted coffee that requires intense roasting.
Bouquet	Fragrance, pleasant aroma.
Bright	Coffee with positive acidity.

Term	Description
Burnt	Bitter taste, due to excess roasting.
Buttery	Describes oily taste in coffee. The taste remaining after drinking is butter-like.
Caramel	A taste of caramelized sugar created during the roasting process that leaves a shade of caramel taste, characterized by slight sweetness – between chocolate and butter.
Carbon	A taste of moldy charcoal resulting from prolonged roasting. The taste remains in the mouth long after drinking.
Chemical/medicinal	Describes a taste of medication or of chemical components.
Chocolatey	Chocolate taste that accompanies some types of coffee, especially from east Africa.
Cinnamon	Coffee with hint of cinnamon-like taste.
Citrusy	A shade of taste typical to certain coffee cultivars, mainly from central America.
Clean	A term used to describe flat coffee without any special flavor.
Cocoa	A sweet taste that recalls the flavor of cocoa.
Complexity	Coffee with a wide range of tastes flavors and mouthfeel, as opposed to monotonic coffee with a single clear taste. Like the difference between a single player and an orchestra.
Cooked	Additional sub-taste, usually due to the use of high roasting temperatures.
Creamy	Oily and smooth coffee.
Dead	Flavorless coffee, without acidity or aroma.
Defects	Unpleasant taste caused by bitterness, moldiness, extremely high acidity or any other reason defined as a coffee defect.
Delicate	Sweet, light and delicate sub-taste that leaves a nice feeling on the tip of the tongue.

Term	Description
Dirty	A moldy taste due to bad drying conditions of coffee beans after harvest.
Dull	Describes a simple coffee without any special characteristics.
Earthy	A wet soil-like sensation in the mouth.
Fermented	A somewhat strange sour, murky taste created by inappropriate treatment during the fermentation process.
Fine cup, good cup	Commonly used by professional cuppers to describe good coffee.
Flat	Coffee without any unique traits, like acidity or bitterness. Described also as poor, weak or dull.
Floral	Coffee cuppers tend to describe the aroma as floral, usually related to specific flowers such as Jasmine, Honeysuckle, etc.
Foreign	Commonly used by professional cuppers to describe uncertain coffee odor faults, mainly due to diseases, fungi, etc.
Foul	Among professional cuppers it's commonly related to a bad smell.
Fragrance	Cuppers use it to describe the aroma of ground coffee before hot water is added.
Fresh	A positive coffee term used to describe clean and aromatic coffee, contrary to old coffee.
Fruity	In some marketed coffee cultivars a shade of fruit aroma can be detected.
Grassy	One of the sub-tastes that's reminiscent of the smell of mowed grass, caused when nitrogen permeates the coffees bean during processing.
Green	Used to describe leaves or a herbal sensation.
Hidey	Used to describe coffee with leather-like flavor.
Intensity	Cuppers use this to describe strong feelings in their mouth. Strong coffee does not always mean good quality!

Term	Description
Malty	One of the aroma components reminiscent of the taste of toast.
Mellow	One of the main taste components that implies mellowness and moderation. The acidity tastes mellow and ripe.
Metallic	Metal-like sub-taste that remains in the mouth after drinking.
Mild	Moderate coffee without any special characteristics.
Muddy	Defines a feeling of particles in the mouth when present in large amounts.
Musty	A rotten smell absorbed in the coffee oil by either muddy water or exposure to dirt.
Neutral	Coffee without pronounced components, even when the coffee is tasty.
Nippy	A sub-taste, describing a special sweetness combined with acidity that creates a sense of nipping on the back of the tongue.
Nutty	Nut smell is one of the most known aroma shades in coffee. Despite its nice smell it may indicate low quality beans.
Oily	A taste created by coffee beans that contain a high level of oil.
Oldish	Green coffee stored for a year, or even more, develop a unique flavor. The flavor is less acidic with pronounced body and some earthy or grassy flavor.
Piquant	A sub-taste, described as a unique positive taste combining high acidity and sweetness, with cinnamon-like or clove shades. Sometime the term spicy is used instead.
Poor	A term used for coffee without aroma.
Pungent	Coffee with strong body and intensity that causes the drinker to feel "a blow" of coffee taste in the mouth.
Rich / Richness	Coffee with good acidity, full body and strong aroma.

Term	Description
Rough	Roughness on the tongue and around the mouth, similar to the taste of unripe fruit – the opposite of round taste.
Round	Coffee that glides smoothly, like oil, through the throat. Another term is "clean."
Rubbery	A negative coffee term describing an unpleasant taste of burnt rubber.
Saltiness	A salty sub-taste spreading in the mouth when drinking coffee.
Sharp	A taste combined of low acidity and high saltiness that usually appears in Robusta that was processed by the dry method.
Smoky	Some coffee cultivars have a smoky taste, but usually, smoky taste happens when the coffee is roasted at a high temperature or when the roaster is out of order and doesn't release the smoke.
Smooth	Used to describe coffee that lacks pungency.
Spicy	Used to describe good coffee with a hint of many sweet spices such as cinnamon, clove, etc.
Stale	A negative taste term describing old roasted coffee.
Stinker	Describes bad coffee with unpleasant smell.
Straw-like	Coffee stored for too long under bad conditions may develop a sub-taste characterized by a strong, straw-like taste.
Strong	A positive coffee term used to describe high flavor, body and aftertaste that remains in the mouth for a long time.
Thin	Coffee with low aroma, flavor, acidity and body.
Toasty	Describes a background taste of toasted bread.
Vapid	A decayed taste, usually because of coffee oxidation due to bad storage conditions. The vapid smell can be sensed even before drinking.

Term	Description
Vinegary	A term to describe an unpleasant acid flavor.
Watery	Describing low quantity of coffee components. Usually indicates low oil content in the beans – the opposite of buttery.
Weak	Opposite of strong – flavorless coffee with weak body and no aftertaste.
Wild	A unique taste characterized by high acidity, which may be too strong for some people.
Winey	Acidic coffee with a taste that's reminiscent of wine.
Woody	Coffee containing a smell of dry wood, usually indicating the green beans were stored for a long period and lost some of its traits.

GLOSSARY

Term	Definition
3-Way Valve	The valve releasing the pressure from the portafilter after preparation of espresso. See term - Portafilter Sneeze.
ABS	Acrylonitrile Butadiene Styrene - A very strong and tough plastic used in many espresso machine housings.
Aged Coffee	Coffee beans that were kept in storage for two or three years before marketing. Aging increases body and reduces acidity.
Air Locked	A phenomenon occurring when the pump in the machine has a stoppage of water flow and air enters the pump. Vibration pumps overcome this condition without intervention. In rotating pumps water should be added to release the block, otherwise air may harm the machine.
Aromatization	A method to permeate aroma into the coffee that has lost its aroma in the production such as with instant coffee and decaffeinating coffee. The aroma and taste are restored by this special treatment.
Arroba	A common weight unit in South America, equal to 25.37 lb (11.5 kg).
Atmosphere	1 Atmosphere = 14.696 PSI = 1.013 Bar.
Baba Budan	The person believed to have smuggled coffee from Ethiopia, who paved the way to its distribution around the world.
Backflush	Part of the cleaning process of espresso machines with a three-way valve (see Periodic Cleaning, page 99).
Bag	Coffee is marketed in the world in jute bags – the common weight is 132 lb (60 kg) but there are other bag weights from 55 to 165 lb (25 – 70 kg).
Bar	1 Bar = 14.5 PSI = 0.987 Atmosphere.

The Term	Definition
Barista	An Italian name for a professional barman specialized in the art of coffee and espresso making.
Beneficio	A Spanish term describing the procedure of cleaning, washing, drying and classifying coffee.
Black Beans	Defective beans that ripen long before the harvest. In many places in the world the amount of black beans in the shipment is used to classify the shipment. Less black beans indicate the coffee was harvested on time.
Blending	Most coffee consumers use a blend of several coffee cultivars. Preparing a good blend is an art that requires accurate balance between the coffee sources and various brewing degrees used to obtain a winning blend. Large companies keep their formula an absolute secret.
Blind Item	Coffee or a coffee blend from an intentionally unidentified source, to hide its origin and get a higher price.
Brewing	The extraction process of coffee substances into hot water.
Brewing Ratio	Water to coffee ratio. The ratio that achieves the ideal mix, for the perfect coffee cup.
Brick Pack	A vacuum packaging invented in 1950 in Germany to store coffee for long term (see Storing, page 51).
Bullhead	Very large coffee beans.
By Defects	Classification term – (See Beans Classification, page 19).
Caturra	A new coffee cultivar, created by hybridization between Arabica and Robusta. This coffee is similar to Arabica in its taste, but is heartier.
Chicory	A plant with blue purple flowers, 1.5-3 ft (0.5-1 m) high, used in food or for brewing. In popular medicine it's used to treat many ailments. The roasted and ground root is used as a coffee replacement.
Coffee Brewer Turbulence	The turbulence created in the filter basket of the espresso machine when water is pressured in. It helps unify the expansion of coffee in the basket.

The Term	Definition
Coffee Year	The coffee year begins October 1 and ends September 30.
Colombian Mild Arabicas	"Colombian Mild Arabicas" is one of four groups that were established in 1965 by the ICO to provide a reliable and consistent price indicator system for different types of coffee. The other groups are "Other Mild Arabicas," "Brazilian and Other Natural Arabicas" and "Robustas."
Crust	When hot water is poured over the coffee grounds during the process of coffee cupping, a thin layer of fine coffee particles floats to the top of the coffee. This is called a crust, and it is removed with a spoon before tasting.
Demitasse	A small cup, used for espresso and Middle Eastern coffee. Sometimes it refers to the coffee itself.
Dispersion Screen	See Shower Screen.
Drink of the Devil	When it first arrived in Europe the Christians called coffee Drink of the Devil. Only at the end of the 16th century Pope Clement the 8th give permission to use it. Legend tells that after he tasted the drink, he decided it shouldn't be only the Muslims' privilege to drink it, and could be Christianized.
E61	In 1961, FAEMA introduced a new espresso machine – the revolutionary E61 – with an electromechanical pump and a thermosiphon system in the grouphead, which kept the head and portafilter hot with hot water flow. . The F61 grouphead system is still used now in many espresso machines.
En Oro	Peeled and cleaned beans.
En Parche	Coffee beans with silver skin.
European Preparation (EP)	See Preparation.
Extra	One of the classifying methods of coffee in Colombia, for instance, extra is the second quality degree.

The Term	Definition
Frequent Average Quality (FAQ)	Coffee quality scoring term.
Filter Holder	The handle into which the filter is inserted. It's made of metal and the heavier it is, the better.
Hard Beans	Classification term indicating medium to high grade beans. Such beans grow at altitudes between 2,600 ft (800 m) to 4,000 ft (1,200 m).
Housing	The external body of espresso machines is one of the important parameters in selecting a machine.
ICO Classifications	Based on four criteria: the country of origin, the crop height, the cultivar and the cultivation method.
ICO Mark	A combination of figures that identifies the coffee shipment, which includes three country code figures, four figures for the exporter or grower code and four figures for the shipment number.
Infusion	The permeation process of water pressure through the coffee to create the extraction.
Light, Medium, Dark Roast, Very Dark Roast	Common names for roasting stages: **Light** – until the first crack, between Cinnamon and American roasting. **Medium** – equivalent to Urban roasting **Dark** – equivalent to full Urban roasting **Very dark** – equivalent to Viennese roasting.
Low Grown	A term used to classify low-grade beans grown at altitudes lower than 4,000 ft (1,200 m) or even under 2,600 ft (800 m).
Macchinetta	Italian name for moka pot. Known also as stove pot espresso maker.
Milk Turbulence	Created when the steam mouthpiece is inserted into the milk jar. It helps whip the milk by injecting air to create bubbles.
Monsooned Coffee	Coffee kept in open storage, exposed to monsoon winds to increase its body and reduce its acidity.

The Term	Definition
Mucilage	The sticky substance that coats the coffee seed when it's released from the cherry.
Napoletana	Also called flip drip moka pot. A special moka pot that's flipped upside down as soon as the water boils, allowing the hot water to percolate through the coffee into the empty reservoir. The result is a strong drink, between press and moka pot.
Nitrogen Flushing	A method used to avoid oxidation of roasted coffee (beans and ground) by filling the packaging with nitrogen.
Over Pressure Valve (OPV)	Most of the pumps in espresso machines produce high pressure. This valve reduces the pressure to 9-10 bar to produce perfect espresso.
Over Extracted	Concentrated coffee or espresso due to use of too much or too finely ground coffee. Some people prefer this type of drink.
Past Crop (PC)	Old coffee.
Percolation	Preparing coffee by streaming hot water through a pored mediator (filter or net).
Percolator	A coffeepot with a filter containing ground coffee, in which the coffee is brewed by dripping almost-boiling water through the coffee (see page 118).
Parchment	A coffee fruit layer that must be removed.
Portafilter	The portafilter is the part of the manual or semi-automatic espresso machine that holds the filter basket. After placing and tamping the ground coffee, the portafilter is inserted into the brew group where the espresso is brewed.
Portafilter Sneeze	In espresso machines without a pressure release system (3-way valve). When espresso is prepared, the developing pressure is about 10 bar, which is released in about 30 sec. Releasing the portafilter too early causes a pressure burst of coffee residue that soils the surroundings.
Pre-Infusion	In some espresso machines a small amount of water is released to produce initial absorption prior to water flow during espresso preparation.

The Term	Definition
Preparation **EP- European Preparation** **USP- U.S.A Preparation**	Classification "By Defects" term. EP or European preparation means that additional hand sorting was done to improve coffee quality. USP or US preparation means less sorting compare to EP.
Pressostat	A small device that controls the pressure in the espresso machine boiler. Some espresso machines use the pressostat to control the temperature in the boiler instead of a thermostat.
Pulp	One of the coffee fruit layers that should be removed during coffee fruit processing. Pulping is also the process of removing the pulp from the fruit (see page 12).
Quenching	Spraying coffee beans with cold water at the end of the roasting process. It's efficient in commercial use, but not recommended for domestic roasting.
Selective Picking	Picking only the ripe cherries during the harvesting season.
Self Priming	Starting the espresso machine pump after air penetrates the pump (see Air Locked).
Shade Coffee	This is a natural method to protect the coffee plants. The coffee bushes are grown beneath taller trees which protect them from the sun and from nesting birds, maintain soil quality, reduce the need for weeding, and aid in pest control.
Shower Screen	Also called Dispersion Screen. The part installed in the head system of espresso machines that spreads the water uniformly over the coffee in the portafilter.
Strictly Hard Beans (SHB)	A term used mainly to classify high quality beans in central America. The quality coffee beans grown at high altitudes develop more slowly, and are harder and better.
Ship Sweepings	Coffee that has absorbed water or humidity during shipment. It's frequently marketed very cheaply.
Silver Skin	One of the coffee fruit layers.

The Term	Definition
Soft Beans	A term to indicate low grade beans, grown at low altitudes under 4,000 ft (1,200 m) or even 2,600 ft (800 m).
Solenoid Valve	An electrical valve that controls the water flow and allows it to flow either from the pump or from the grouphead.
Stall(ing)	A process in which the water doesn't flow through the coffee. It happens when the grind is too fine or when the espresso machine is defective and doesn't create pressure.
Steeping	Preparing a coffee drink by soaking ground coffee in hot water.
Stewed	Re-heating coffee – it causes a loss of coffee aroma.
Strip Picking	Picking all the coffee fruit at once by hand or by machine.
Strong Coffee	The term "strong coffee" relates to coffee beverage with high bitterness. It can be obtained by the presence of more Robusta or by very dark roasting.
Substitutes	Alternatives to coffee like chicory.
Sultana Coffee	The peel of the dry coffee cherry.
Sweated Coffee	A method using steam to change green beans to a darker color, with the intention to forge a better appearance.
Taste Receptors	Tasting cells concentrated in the mouth and on the tongue, allowing us to detect thousands of tastes.
Thermosiphon	Water flow due to temperature gradient, used in espresso machines with a heat exchanger. Specifically grouphead E61 uses this physical phenomenon to warm the portafilter.
The Black Frost	On July 17, 1975 a three day severe frost, called the "Black Frost" the most severe in the modern era, hit Brazil and destroyed about one third of the coffee fruit. The price of Brazilian coffee soared. The ICO site has logged all natural world coffee crises in the last century.

The Term	Definition
Total Dissolved Solids (TDS)	The measured amount of solids dissolved in brewed, filtered coffee, is between 1-1.5%, depending on the amount of coffee, brewing time, grind coarseness and water temperature.
Triage	A term used to describe sorting criteria of coffee beans – whole, half-broken and broken.
Umami	In 1907 Kikunae Ikeda, a Japanese professor, found that monosodium glutamate makes food taste better and named the special flavor "umami." We call it the fifth taste (in addition to the four basic taste components - sour, bitter, sweet and salty).
Under Extracted	Coarsely ground, low temperature, small amount of coffee or low water pressure resulting in poor extraction of coffee components.

USEFUL LINKS

Searching Google for coffee yields more than 1 billion resources. The following table represents my own personal choices for good coffee sites. The Internet is a dynamic medium, and there are always new sites, some change their address, some remove the information from the net and some close down.

The information presented here was collected on March, 2015.

I would be happy to receive comments on any change or inaccuracy in the information and/or on any sites you'd like to share.

Internet address	Description
International Coffee Organization (ICO) **www.ico.org**	One of the main coffee organizations, the ICO, established in 1963, is located in London and deals with the advancement of coffee and its quality. The organization is devoted to improving the coffee economy by coordinating between members, (exporting and importing countries) administering coffee policy agreements and government priorities. The organization website supplies information about its activities and on other coffee topics – the coffee tree, cultivation, data on coffee commerce in recent years and more.
Specialty Coffee Association of America (SCAA) **www.scaa.org**	SCAA is a non-profit organization devoted to excellence, maintaining standards of retailers, roasters, exporters, importers and coffee equipment producers. It has several sub-organizations such as the Roasters Guild and others, and has representatives around the world. It also organizes worldwide barista competitions.
Specialty Coffee Association of Europe **www.scae.com**	The SCAE is the European branch of the SCAA. The site provides information about coffee related courses and events. It also contains a list of representatives in each country.

Internet address	Description
Association Scientifique, Internationale du Café **www.asic-cafe.org**	ASIC, the coffee Sciences International Organization. Based in Paris. A "meeting place" for professional coffee scientists and technologists from all over the world to exchange ideas and scientific knowledge on coffee. The main topics ASIC deal with are coffee agronomy, chemistry, technology, physiological effects, packaging, storage, etc. Its members receive technological articles and participate in conferences every second year.
British Coffee Association (BCA) **www. britishcoffeeassociation.org**	The British Coffee Association website contains information about related objectives: health, history and coffee processing. On this site, as in other organizational sites, there's a blocked area for members only.
Coffee Association of Canada **www.coffeeassoc.com**	The Coffee Association of Canada is the national trade association representing the coffee industry in Canada.
Coffee kids (org) **www.coffeekids.org**	A nonprofit organization that was founded in 1988 by Bill Fishbein and colleagues who met on a trip and saw the impoverished state of coffee farmers' children. Their aim is to help coffee farmers improve the quality of their coffee as well as their living conditions. The association is aided by donations and selling shirts and cups. It's not connected in any way to the coffeekid.com site.
Coffee Quality Institute **www.coffeeinstitute.org**	The Coffee Quality Institute (CQI), founded in 1996, is a nonprofit educational and international research organization, aiming mainly to improve the quality of marketed coffee and the lives of the people who produce it. Originally, it was named Specialty Coffee Institute, and the name and address of the site were changed recently to reflect the essence of the organization.
Coffee Research **www.coffeeresearch.org**	An information site dedicated to coffee education with comprehensive coverage on coffee. It's one of the largest coffee information resource sites (more than 300 pages) dealing with coffee that contains almost all the issues related to coffee: harvest, roasting, brewing, health, consumption, world trade and more. There's also a huge collection of pictures and videos related to coffee.

Internet address	Description
E.S.E. **www.esesystem.com**	Pod standardization site.
Eastern African Fine Coffees Association (AFCA) **www.eafca.org**	The AFCA, is a nonprofit, nonpolitical member-driven association established in 2000 in Uganda, representing growers, exporters, importers, roasters and all entities involved in coffee trading. The association incorporates 11 countries from the east of Africa – Burundi, The DR of the Congo, Ethiopia, Kenya, Malawi, Rwanda, South Africa, Tanzania, Uganda, Zambia and Zimbabwe. It aims to improve the ability of members to compete and increase their profits. The site presents the activities of the AFCA and various coffee cultivars grown in these countries. Membership requires subscription and payment and provides much information.
Fair Trade USA **www.fairtradeamerica.org** Fair Trade International **www.fairtrade.net**	Fair Trade is an organized social movement attempting to help farmers and farm workers improve their quality of life by getting better and fair pricing for their products (coffee, tea, bananas, etc.). The organization controls high pricing, by adding Fair Trade labeling on their products. There are several Fair Trade organizations, the two major ones are Fair Trade International and Fair Trade USA that was part of the international organization but withdrew in 2011 to conduct their own activity. Recently, many coffee companies have demanded to see the "Fair Trade" certificate before purchasing products.
IndexMundi **www.indexmundi.com**	Select: agriculture > green coffee IndexMundi is a data portal that gathers facts and statistics from multiple sources about green coffee beans and turns them into easy to use visuals.
Institute for Scientific Information on Coffee **www.coffeeandhealth.org**	The Institute for Scientific Information on Coffee (ISIC) is a nonprofit organization founded in 1990 dedicated to scientific research on coffee, caffeine and health. The organization activities focus on studying scientific matters related to coffee and health, collecting scientific research and information on coffee and health from all over the world, supporting scientific research and distributing knowledge on those topics. Members of the organization are seven major European coffee companies. The ISIC website provides the latest reliable data on research finding on coffee caffeine and health.

Internet address	Description
National Coffee Association of U.S.A. (NCA) **www.ncausa.org**	The National USA coffee trade association was established in 1911. It aims to provide a strategic advantage in the global marketplace to their members by leading research on coffee and its consumption. The site contains information about the association and coming events, as well as the story of coffee – from the field to the cup – including storage, roasting and more.
Rainforest Alliance **www.rainforest-alliance.org**	In 1986 Daniel Katz and other members established a volunteer's organization "The Rainforest Alliance" that aims to preserve the ecological balance in the world from contamination and prevents the destruction of rain forests around the world by fostering natural agriculture without artificial intervention. The volunteers began to help farmers preserve natural processing methods. Coffee is one of the crops in areas with high conservation priorities and therefore the alliance promotes coffee purchasing with "Rainforest Alliance" certificate.
The Alliance for Coffee Excellence (ACE) Inc **www.allianceforcoffeee xcellence.org/en/**	In 1999 a group of coffee growers decided to conduct a fair competition to find out who produces the best coffee. The Alliance for Coffee Excellence, (ACE) Inc., founded in 2002 is a non-profit organization that manages and executes the "Cup of Excellence" program all over the world. Coffee growers send their coffee where it is tasted and graded by experts and then ACE conducts an auction, selling the coffee to the highest bidder. The "Cup of Excellence" winners sell their coffee at a very high price compared to the rest of the market. The ACE website shows the competition results and auctions dates. One can watch the auction on-line and even purchase coffee.
The Roasters Guild **www.roastersguild.org**	This is a sub-association of SCAA aiming to organize expert roasters and to improve roasting skills. They promote standards, investigations and various activities for the benefit of coffee roasters. Membership enables notification on upcoming events.
United States Department of Agriculture **www.fas.usda.gov/ commodities/coffee**	(USDA) United States Department of Agriculture report official data on U.S. and global trade, production, consumption and stocks, as well as analysis of developments affecting world trade in coffee, and World Markets and Trade reports.

Internet address	Description
UTZ Kapeh **www.utzcertified.org**	The UTZ organization was established in 1992 in cooperation by the Guatemalan coffee growers and the Dutch coffee roasting company Ahold, to create an independent control and monitoring system and to ensure the consumer full credibility and transparency of the coffee processing chain: growing, harvesting, cultivation, transportation, roasting and coffee preparation.
World Coffee Events (Championship) **www.worldcoffeeevents.org**	World Coffee Events (WCE) was founded by the SCAA and SCAE to be the premier producer of events for the coffee community worldwide. Their mission is to develop events that engage the specialty in the coffee community and promote coffee excellence. The WCE organizes events such as the World Barista Championship, World Latte Art Championship and others.
Brazil Specialty Coffee Association (BSCA) **www.bsca.com.br**	The Brazil Specialty Coffee Association (BSCA) is a non-profit founded in 1991 by 12 Brazilian coffee producers who wanted to promote quality coffee – the very best of Cafés do Brazil. The BSCA deals with techniques of quality control, coffee excellence standards, monitoring and quality control of coffee specialty and more. Members can certify their coffee quality with the BSCA seal. Members can also participate in national and international events, seminars, workshops, conferences, fairs, etc.
"Espresso! My Espresso!" **www.espressomy espresso.com**	Ongoing Internet Novelette by coffee addict Randy Glass.
Caffeine Archive **www.caffeinearchive.com**	A website with coffee reference and information.
Coffee Forums **www.coffeeforums.com** **www.coffeeforums.co.uk**	Coffee forums from US and UK.
Coffee Hits **www.coffeehits.com**	This site ranks internet coffee sites. It provides links and classifies 150 coffee sites, most of which are online shops. There's a constant competition between various sites to get to the top of the list.

Internet address	Description
Coffee Kid **www.coffeekid.com**	An informational site founded by Mark Prince from Vancouver, Canada. It contains essential and basic knowledge on coffee. There's no connection between this site and coffeekids.org.
Coffee Review **www.coffeereview.com**	A very powerful site founded by coffee experts Kenneth Davids and Ron Walters, who rate coffee and publish the results. Because many companies want to receive a good review it has become a very popular site. It includes articles on coffee tasting and information on coffee quality all over the world.
coffeefaq **www.coffeefaq.com**	A website containing common Information, questions and answers on coffee and caffeine, etc.
CoffeeGeek **www.coffeegeek.com**	A website that educates the coffee and espresso loving public, and entertains and informs coffee fans. Provides a lots of information on coffee machines, grinders and other information on homemade coffee. It compares various accessories and contains reviews and articles by members, fans and professionals.
Daily Coffee News **www.dailycoffeenews.com**	Daily Coffee News is the news source for specialty coffee professionals.
Espresso Top 50 **www.espressotop50.com**	Website that classifies and rates a list of 150 best espresso sites.
Home-Barista **www.home-barista.com**	Coffee forum. You can get a lot of information from fans and professionals. Recommended for those who wanted to expand their coffee knowledge.
http://www.supremo.be	A trading Belgian company with a lot of data on coffee producing countries.
I need coffee **www.ineedcoffee.com**	A coffee information website. Michael Allen Smith, a coffee groupie, launched the site in 1999 as an open platform for coffee fans and professionals to publish favorite beverages.

Internet address	Description
National Geographic **www.nationalgeographic.com/coffee**	The coffee section of the National Geographic contains descriptions of coffee around the world, including maps of each country and basic information on coffee.
Quality Assurance International (QAI) **www.qai-inc.com**	A certifying agency for certified organic coffee growers.
Roast Magazine **www.roastmagazine.com** Fresh Cup Magazine **http://www.freshcup.com/** Barista Magazine **http://baristamagazine.com/** Tea And Coffee **http://www.teaandcoffee.net/**	Well-known online coffee magazines favored by those in the coffee industry.
Seattle Coffee Gear **www.seattlecoffeegear.com**	Commercial site with lots of information relevant to the coffee machine and a huge amount of training videos.
Sweet Marias **www.sweetmarias.com**	One of the best green coffee information sites.
The National Federation of Coffee Growers of Colombia **www.juanvaldez.com**	The official National Federation of Coffee Growers of Colombia website is represented by the Juan Valdez brand established in 1927 to improve Colombian coffee quality and the reliability of the coffee commerce.
Coffee talk **www.coffeetalk.com**	A daily coffee news and information website.
MTC Group **www.mtcgroup.com.au/**	MTC Group is an International specialty coffee importer and trader with direct relationships at origin, working at producer and mill level to source and improve coffees at the farm gate.
Animal coffee - Kopi Luwak **www.animalcoffee.com**	A roasting house based in Bali, Indonesia. A reliable wild civets kopi luwak source. They do not farm or cultivate the civets. The coffee they supply is from Sumatra, Java and Borneo collecting plants.

Most of the color pictures from this book can be found at

www.coffee-lovers-guide.com

Made in the USA
Middletown, DE
08 March 2021